In Exmoor Countrie

In this series

Down Partymoor Way

In Exmoor Countrie

Pen and ink drawings of the Exmoor National Park

Design, illustration and script
PENNY HOUSDEN

Original text and verse
MARY HOUSDEN

Foreword
SIR JOHN ACLAND, 16th Baronet

Piles Mill
near Allerford

Penmarran

First published in Great Britain 1996/7 by
Penmarran Publishing
60 Argyll Road
Pennsylvania, Exeter
Devon EX4 4RY

British Library Cataloguing~in~Publication Data

A catalogue record for this book is
available from the British Library

ISBN 1 872852 01 7

Copies of this and other books published by Penmarran can be
obtained direct from the publisher at the above address.

Printed and bound by
BPC Wheatons Ltd
Hennock Road
Marsh Barton
Exeter EX2 8RP

Contents

Oare Water

Foreword

I wish this book had been written some thirty or forty years earlier. It would have tempted me off the straight and narrow, which in my case consisted of regular journeys from Killerton to Holnicote, never deviating from the Exe Valley until Wheddon Cross. The style and content of 'In Exmoor Countrie' discourage such single-mindedness. Instead, one is stimulated to adopt a leisurely pace and to explore through lanes or over moorland. One's only other needs are the Ordnance Survey map and time. How easy it would be to become addicted, ticking off the pages much as Scottish hill walkers tick off the Munroes.

Penny and Mary Housden deserve our warmest congratulations. I am sure that many of their readers will be reminded of A. Wainwright's guides to the Lake District. The combination of perfect pen and ink drawings with beautiful hand-written text brought the Lake District to life for me and I am sure that this book will do the same for very many readers who want to know the secrets of Exmoor.

SIR JOHN ACLAND
16th Baronet

Landacre
Bridge

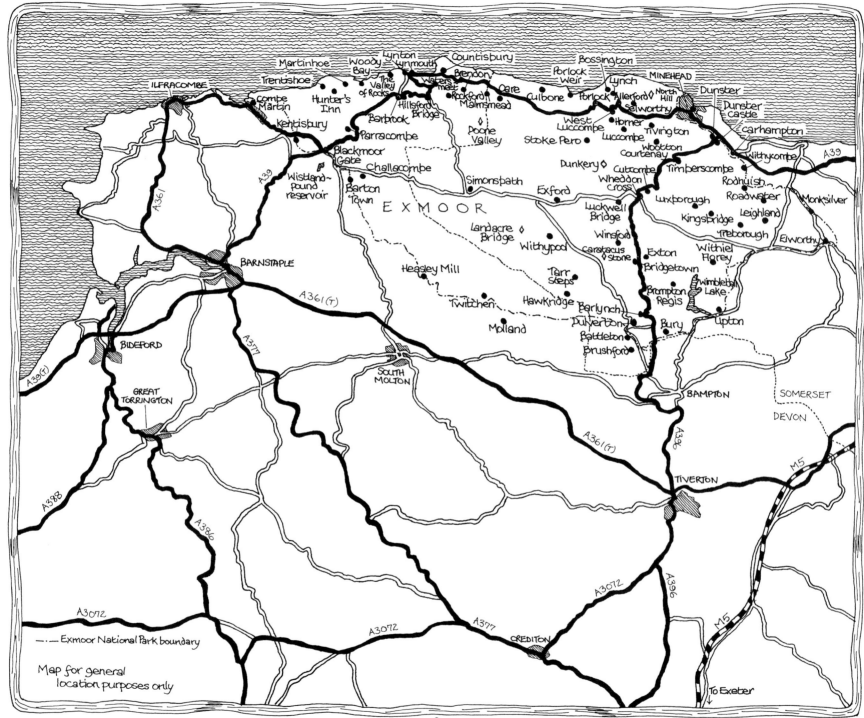

Introduction

Designated a National Park in 1954, Exmoor lies one third in Devon and two thirds in Somerset, every acre of which is privately owned or belongs to a corporate concern such as the National Trust or the Somerset County Council. Every step taken on the Moor, and there are 600 miles of public foot~paths, is at the courtesy of someone.

Exmoor presents such a diversity of aspects that it can mean different things to different people. For some it is the purple~heathered hills and tree~filled valleys, for others the precipitous jagged cliffs and coastal heathlands. Some think of it in terms of the white~scarred trek up to Dunkery Beacon, the highest spot on Exmoor, others the lovely Doone Valley with its lonesome combes. It could mean a day out in Dunster and a view of the castle, picnics at Landacre Bridge, cream teas at Winsford, a walk through the splendid oakwoods of Horner, or the revitalizing wonderment of Tarr Steps or Watersmeet.

It is all these things and much, much more ~ rocky shores, beech~hedged lanes, an abundance of wild flora and fauna, the roaming mealy~mouthed ponies, and if you're lucky, a glorious glimpse of the elusive red deer whose habitat it has been since prehistoric times. Reminders of ancient man abound in the surrounding hills in the many barrows and tumuli and in the remains of defensive iron~age hillforts, while coursing throughout is an interlacing network of singing rivers and merry streams that symbolizes the very life~blood of the Moor. Equally delightful is the host of enchanting towns, villages and hamlets enfolded in the landscape whose well~preserved cottages and medieval buildings, encompassed by a magnificence of hills, give Exmoor its air of constancy.

Here then, in pen and ink illustration are features of these communities in this, the Exmoor National Park, with a little of their immediate history.

The dovecote at Blackford

I first heard tell of a wondrous land
As a child at my Mother's knee,
Where the sky was bluer than anywhere else
And the hills bowed down to the sea;
Where rustic lanes led to beautiful sights,
And combes ran wild with flowers,
And the red deer roamed, and the foxes played,
And the birds sang in treetop bowers;
Where it gave the illusion of time holding still,
Though rich in a past lingering on,
By sun-sparkled waters of onward intent
Troubles floated away and were gone;
When I came of age I searched till I found
This place tucked away in my heart,
It turned out to be in Exmoor Countrie,
Nature's wonderful work of art.

Badgworthy
Water

NORTHERN EXMOOR

Northern Exmoor

TRENTISHOE
HUNTER'S INN
MARTINHOE
WOODY BAY
LYNTON
LYNMOUTH
THE VALLEY OF ROCKS
WATERSMEET
COUNTISBURY
A39
CULBONE
PORLOCK WEIR
BOSSINGTON
LYNCH
NORTH HILL
MINEHEAD
PORLOCK
ALLERFORD
SELWORTHY
COMBE MARTIN
A399
B3343
A39
A39
B3223
A39
A396

The Whit Stones on Porlock Hill

Toll cottage at Worthy near Porlock Weir

Memorial hut on North Hill

Map for location purposes only

13

Combe Martin

It's a long winding road to the harbour
Where tall cliffs rise out of the ocean
And holiday crowds watch the small craft
Bob at anchor ~ like poetry in motion.

Not strictly within the confines of the Exmoor National Park but lying at its western fringe on the north Devon coast, Combe Martin is popular as a holiday centre, having a picturesque harbour and some magnificent scenery. It was named after Martin de Turon, friend of William the Conqueror. The village street of some two miles is claimed to be the longest in Britain, flanked on either side by mostly Victorian houses. To the east of the village soar the Little Hangman and Great Hangman cliffs reaching to 1,044 feet, and from where can be seen on a clear day marvellous views across the Bristol Channel to the Welsh coastline and mountains.

Combe Martin has a long history of silver mining lasting from the end of the 13th century up to 1875 and adits and shafts abound in the district, with tunnels running under the main street.

Because the valley is a warm and fertile area it is notable for its abundant strawberry growing and vegetable produce, supplying to Ilfracombe and Lynton, as well as exporting. At one time hemp was grown from which shoemakers' thread was spun.

The church of St. Peter ad Vincula, in pink sandstone, is mostly of 15th century date, as is the 99~foot battlemented tower, with a south porch built in 1724.

An interestingly~shaped inn the 'Pack o' Cards' is reputed to have been built by a man who had won a fortune at cards, and visitors find it amusing to try and count the original 13 doors and 52 win~ dows representing the number of cards in a suit and in the pack.

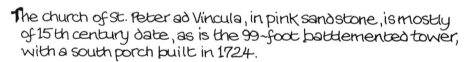

Lester Point, at the entrance to the harbour ▶

Trentishoe

In the shelter of its cleave
This tiny hamlet weathers on
Content to live what folk believe
The Good Life, which for some has gone.

Bounded on three sides by 1,000~foot high wooded cliffs, this small coastal settlement has diminished in population over the years. In 1891 the census recorded 96 persons, but by the 1961 census the figure had fallen to 47. Farms and cottages disappeared, as did the corn mill, the smithy's forge, and an inn, until today there is only a small cluster of houses and the small stone church of St. Peter nestling in the hollow of its cleave known as Peter's Rock.

One of the smallest parish churches in Devon, it holds the Royal Arms of George V dated 1911, and has an interesting musicians' gallery, but not since 1859 has it had a resident rector. Although parish regis~ters were ordered to be kept by an act of Parliament in 1538, the first volume at Trentishoe starts from 1697, indicating that an earlier one must have been lost. In the churchyard are graves of un~known persons that have been washed ashore; there is one who fought aboard H.M.S. Victory at the Battle of Trafalgar, and a centenarian who died in 1893, the last of the local band of smugglers.

Church of
St. Peter

R.D. Blackmore had associations with this lovely haven, having, in 1864, published his first novel 'Clara Vaughan' which was set in Trentishoe, opening in the year 1842. A branch of the Blackmore family had lived in the parish during the 18th century and a son of the Rev. Morgan Cooke, rector of Trentishoe had married a sister of Blackmore's great~grandfather.

To the west are the twin crests of Holdstone and Trentishoe Down, both showing grave~mounds or barrows, and which are linked by a pathway. The Somerset and North Devon Coast path skirts the cliffs around Trentishoe.

The hamlet of Trentishoe ▶

Penny Housden

Hunter's Inn

Anglers, artists, writers, walkers,
Naturalists, birdwatchers too,
Make this woodland inn their haven
While exploring life anew.

About one mile inland, between the hamlets of Trentishoe and Martinhoe, the picturesque Hunter's Inn has its home in the beautiful Heddon Valley through which the river runs to the sea. A favourite haunt of a variety of visitors, all succumb to the beauty of the wild scenery encompassing this headland: rolling hills, wooded combes, precipitous cliffs, rough winding tracks over moor and down. In Henry Williamson's 'The Old Stag', the story reaches an exciting climax when, after a 6-hour chase, the stag plunges dramatically into the sea at Heddon's Mouth.

Formerly on this site a thatched cottage was in situ where farmers and labourers alike would meet and jollify over a pint of ale in their leisure time. Lack of transport in those days would preclude them from the long haul into towns. The farmer's wife would serve them from a barrel of beer in the large kitchen which was 'the bar', and when one barrel became empty another was fetched in the farm cart from Ilfracombe, entailing a day's trip on the rough roads.

A family by the name of Berry became tenants in 1868, farming the surrounding land, and as they became popular they drew in visitors from seaside towns. The cottage expanded, new buildings were added, eventually becoming an inn in the true sense. On a windy day in 1895 the thatched roof caught fire, reducing the inn to ruins within minutes. Foundations of the present inn, with tiled roof, were laid the following year, but as most of the materials had to be brought by wagon from Landkey, the building took several years to complete. By that time, because the Heddon Valley had become known as 'The Switzerland of England', the new owner, Colonel Lake, modelled the new buildings on a Swiss chalet.

Hunter's Inn ▶

18

Martinhoe

A coastal village set on moorland heights
  By jagged cliffs enduring, beetle~browed,
The ocean moods and wild Atlantic winds
  With which this coastline is so well endowed.

A coastal village where heathery moorland runs down to craggy cliffs and the cliffs hang perilously over the sea. Part of a magnificent coastline stretching from The Valley of Rocks to Woody Bay where it eventually falls to the sea at Heddon's Mouth to the north~west.

Remote, and with a palpable sense of history, Martinhoe is but a hamlet, having few houses and farms. Martinhoe Manor was recorded in Domesday, as was Killington, now a farm. The little stone church, dedicated to St. Martin, stands firm and defiant against the western gales. From earliest times up to the 17th century coastal villages were always open to attack from overseas marauders and it was natural for people to take refuge in their churches. There appears to have been a chapel on this site since Saxon times, with substantial rebuilding in Norman times (the original font is now in St. Petrock's church at Parracombe), but not until about AD 1200 was it built in the form recognised today. Further extensive restoration took place in the last century. The tower holds two ancient bells.

In the 1870s curate James Harrington, in yellow knee~breeches and studded boots, rode about the parishes preaching and visiting the sick. He later joined the Church Missionary Society, was sent to East Africa, and in 1884 after being consecrated Bishop set off for what is now Uganda. The native King, fearing his influence, had him murdered near the banks of Lake Victoria.

On Martinhoe Beacon are remains of a Roman fort built about AD 50, said to have been occupied by a garrison of 80 soldiers (in wooden barracks as opposed to tents), on lookout for the warlike Silures of South Wales. In 1960/1 this fort was excavated by archaeologists ~ the furnace, ovens, weapons, pottery and coins found can be seen in Barnstaple's museum.

St. Martin's church ▶

Woody Bay

When the tide elopes beneath undercut slopes
There's an apron of rock~strewn shore,
When invading seas overpower with ease
You can hear the echoes roar.

The high and wooded coastline embracing this bay of untold beauty a few miles west of Lynton is some of the finest in the Exmoor National Park, together with the surrounding area of outstanding scenery, the property of the National Trust since 1965.

The beach at Woody Bay can only be reached on foot down a steep gradient where a small stretch of rock~strewn sand is inevitably cut off at high tide, and visitors should avoid being stranded. Around 1895 a syndicate was formed to develop the bay. A pier was built where paddle~steamers could bring day~trippers, but when it was destroyed in a storm a few years later all further schemes were abandoned.

There are many attractive houses dotted about in the grandeur of the oak~wooded slopes, facing a sea of many moods and aspects, an ever~changing scene, where gulls, kittiwakes and fulmars glide and wheel around the bay. On the cliff-side the Woody Bay Hotel is a welcome oasis in the landscape. On private land there is evidence of a Roman fortlet from AD 58 which served as a lookout across the Bristol Channel, but all that is left are concentric circular banks and ditches. From a lower level can be seen the cascade from the Hollow Brook which tumbles down the cliff reaching the shore through replanted woodland.

In the days of the Lynton to Barnstaple narrow~gauge rail~way ~from 1898 to 1935 ~ the line, following the contours of the cliffs through some magnificent scenery, reached its highest peak, 1,000 feet, at Woody Bay.

The roads out of Woody Bay with their hairpin bends are considered comparable to Swiss mountain roads.

Woody Bay
Hotel

Grandeur of the bay ▶

The Valley of Rocks

In some primeval time these rock formations,
Thrown up by great convulsions of the land,
Impress the eye with structural variations,
Inscribe the mind with legendary hand.

In a 1½ mile stretch from Lynton in the east to Wringcliff Bay in the west, and running parallel to the coast, this dry valley of rugged tors is thought to have been carved by water, representing the old valley of the Lyn river before coastal erosion altered its course. The Valley is owned by Lynton Town Council and can be reached either by the Valley road from Lynton or by the North Walk from Lynton.

Many of the rock piles have names, and from their heights can be enjoyed extensive views along the coast and across the Bristol Channel to Wales. 'Castle Rock' rising to just under 800 feet has at its pinnacle a gap in the rock which, viewed against the sky, shows the outline of a lady in a long white dress and bonnet and carrying a tray, and is known as 'The White Lady'. 'Rugged Jack', as legend goes, is named after a Lynton lad called Jack who, missing church one Sunday to skylark in the valley with his friends, was visited by the devil who claimed them for his own by transforming them into rocks. 'Chimney Rock' is said to have been used by wreckers in the 18th century on which to light a beacon to lure ships on to the rocks.

The Devil's
Cheese Ring

'The Devil's Cheese Ring' on the southern slope of the Valley is so named because it resembles an old-fashioned cheese press. It was amongst these rocks that old Mother Meldrum the wise woman in 'Lorna Doone' lived in a cave in the winter.

Ferral goats can be seen from time to time clambering the rocks, and it was on Castle Rock that Blackmore's John Ridd witnessed the bitter fight between a sheep and a goat.

The adjoining Lee Abbey was built in 1850 on the site of Ley Manor where the De Wichehalse family lived for many years.

The sweep of the Valley of Rocks ▶

Perry Housden

Linked to its sister village below
  By the rivers Lyn that swiftly flow,
High on its hill it guards the past,
    There is no forgetting, memories last.

Located on a cliff 500 feet above its twin village of Lynmouth, and once an agricultural and fishing community, Lynton now depends for its livelihood on the tourist trade. Although old cottages line the back streets, Victorian and Edwardian architecture predominates, due to the influx in the 19th century of notable people who came and built themselves houses. Amongst them was the benefactor Sir George Newnes the publisher who, in 1881, launched the magazine 'Tit-bits'. He financed the building of the Town Hall at a cost of £20,000, officially opened by his friend Sir Arthur Conan Doyle.

The difficulty of access between the two villages prompted Sir George to sponsor a local engineer, Mr Bob Jones, in the construction of a cliff railway. Exploiting a natural crevice in the cliff it was begun in 1887 and was opened on Easter Monday 1890, the first of its kind in England. The railway 'lift', which is still operating, is 900 feet in length with a 1 in 1¾ gradient. The two cars (each carrying 20 passengers) are controlled by water tanks containing 500 gallons apiece.

The cliff railway ascending to Lynton

A narrow-gauge railway, from Lynton to Barnstaple was completed and opened in 1898, but by 1935 the decreasing number of passengers made it unviable and it was considered a sad day when it closed. Another incredible innovation was electric light which reached the village in 1890 without ever having gas which was still prevalent in London. A museum by the carpark depicts life in the area over the centuries, displaying tools and implements. The Roman Catholic church of St. Mary's in Lee Road has an altar from Rome and a font of blue marble.

Travel by horse-drawn coaches was at its peak around 1880 - the two main coaching routes being from Lynton to Barnstaple, and Lynton to Minehead; these later overtaken by the charabanc.

Lynton's main street ▶

Penny Housden

Lynmouth

Beneath majestic cliffs clear waters tumble to the sea
Indicating not a whit the force that they could be,
Cottages of quaint design, hotels in scenic wonder
Serve visitors who come to view the place once rent asunder.

Nestling 500 feet beneath its twin village of Lynton, and where the two rivers, the East Lyn in its rocky ravine, the West Lyn in its densely-wooded valley, converge before rushing the last few hundred yards into the sea, Lynmouth is flanked by precipitous cliffs and spectacular scenery that draws holiday-makers from all over the world. For centuries this little fishing village and harbour had relied on its herring and pilchard fisheries for survival, with a small coastal trade coming in and going out, but it remained comparatively remote and undiscovered until the Napoleonic Wars closed the continent to English visitors who then had to look elsewhere for enjoyment. As the number of summer and honeymooning visitors increased, more shops and hotels were built and so the fishing industry declined and tourism thrived.

On the little quay the Rhenish Tower, an imitation of the towers on the Rhine, built by a General Rawdon early in the 19th century, is a monument whose beacon flare in a tar barrel once guided the men at sea. The lofty contour of Countisbury Hill, with its cliff-hugging road, rises to a majestic 1,000 feet; running south-east is the beautiful valley of the East Lyn. In the village the steep path of Mars Hill with its attractive cottages leads up towards Lynton.

All the world knows of that black Friday night of 15 August 1952 when, after a prolonged period of torrential rain, the East and West Lyn streams became roaring torrents as an estimated 90 million tons of water, and 100,000 tons of boulders and debris descended on the little town demolishing bridges, hotels, houses and the tower, leaving a death toll of 34. Worldwide contributions to a relief fund raised £1,336,425, the village rebuilt by June 1954, measures taken to avoid repetition of such a tragedy.

From Lynmouth to Ivybridge in South Devon runs the Two Moors Way, passing through Exmoor and Dartmoor, 102 miles of rural footpaths.

The Rhenish Tower

Lynmouth houses overlooking the East Lyn ▶

Watersmeet

Deep in the vale the three rivers converge
  Over time~worn boulders they leap and surge,
Cascading down in a fury of sound
  Following a conflict course, seaward bound.

Less than a mile south of its coastal neighbour, Countisbury, and a pleasant walk from Lynmouth, the beauty spot of Watersmeet lies in a natural and dramatic landscape of rapid rivers, steep densely~wood~ed hillsides, high farmland, and some open moor. The estate is administered by the National Trust whose property it is, and who have provided car parks in the area for the many visitors who call.

Down in the gorge overhung by a canopy of leaves, at the very heart of Watersmeet, the East Lyn river cascades and leaps over giant boulders in an echoing reverberation of sound, dashing wildly under the Chiselcombe footbridge in its hurry down the winding valley to meet up with the West Lyn, and thence to the sea. Two streams join up with the East Lyn at Watersmeet, Hoaroak Water and Farley Water, which, from their source on the windswept plateau of The Chains, run parallel from Exe Plain towards Hillsford Bridge where they converge before spilling into the East Lyn.

On the banks of the river Watersmeet House has stood since 1830, built by the Halliday family as a fishing and hunting lodge, but now accommodating a rest~aurant and gift shop run by the National Trust. The stone to build the house was extracted from the quarry a little distance up the valley. Nearby there is a restored lime kiln where the limestone used to arrive from South Wales, a surprising distance from the coast. Attempts were made during the last century to extract iron ore, without success. Across the river from the house the horizontal shaft of the mine can still be seen.

On the lawn by the house an impressive Monterey Pine spr~eads its shade, although the woods are mainly of sessile oak and a scattering of the Devon whitebeam.

Watersmeet House in its setting ▶

30

Penny Housden

Countisbury

A hamlet nestling on a hill
Knows well its beauteous heights,
The little church with head in cloud
Rests on its heavenly sights.

Consisting only of a church, a few cottages, and a 16th century inn, Countisbury, with its beautiful coastal and inland scenery, lies on the ancient ridge-road between Lynmouth and Porlock. The Exmoor Sandpiper Inn was originally called The Blue Ball. In the great sailing days a blue ball would be hoisted by the coastguard to signal a safe harbour. 'Countisbury' is said to mean 'the camp on the headland' derived from the Iron Age fort on Wind Hill. Here Odda of Devon defeated the Danes in AD 878. The lighthouse at Fore land Point, the most northerly point of Devon, was built in 1900 and its light, in clear weather, can be seen for 26 miles. The only access to a beach is at Sillery Sands, from a coast path.

In January 1899 the hamlet was witness to an unprecedented sight when the Lynmouth lifeboat 'Louisa', unable to be launched to a ship in distress because of a great storm raging at Lynmouth that night, was hauled 1,000 feet up the treacherous Countisbury Hill on its way to Porlock Weir; 100 men and 20 horses, many falling by the wayside, pushed and pulled the lifeboat on its carriage for 15 miles with many difficulties, once having to demolish a cottage wall that was in the way, finally to descend the dreaded Porlock Hill. It took 11 hours, but when it was eventually launched at 8 a.m. and reached the S.S. Forest Hall, help from the tug 'Jollife' was already under way.

The church of St. John the Evangelist is the parish church of Lynmouth, Watersmeet and Countisbury, the roof having been completely restored in 1972. The wall-mounted bell-clappers inside were removed from the bell tower in 1964 when the bells were sold to pay for repairs. In the churchyard lie most of the crew of that epic lifeboat launch of 1899.

A leaning chimney stack

A view of Countisbury from the Common ►

Culbone

Steadfast down the centuries
This little house of prayer
Stands tribute to the many souls
Who lived and laboured there.

Over 400 feet high in a densely wooded combe near to coastal waters this remote hamlet of a church and two houses is set in tranquil surroundings, the only sound a murmuring stream that makes its way down to the shore. At only 35 feet long by 12 feet 4 inches wide and dating from around 1280, the old rubble-stone church has the distinction of being the smallest parish church in England, and is complete with porch, nave, a Norman font, and a carved oak chancel screen. Its short slated spire is purported to have blown off the top of Porlock's (truncated) church spire during a storm! Originally called Kitnor, derived from the Saxon 'Cyta' and 'Oare' ~ a cave by the sea ~ Culbone had, by the end of the 18th century, taken its name from the Celtic missionary from Wales, St. Beuno, to whom the church is dedicated, a distortion of 'Kil Beun' ~ the church of St. Beuno.

Because of its isolation Culbone became an enclosure for outcasts, and mainly served as a prison settlement. In 1544 it became a leper colony, and in 1720 prisoners of war lived in the woods as charcoal burners, the charcoal being in demand as fuel for England's industries. In later years local sawyers supplied the oak for shipbuilding.

The gatehouse

Registers show that in 1831, at the peak of Culbone's population, 62 people lived in 11 houses, and in 1901 34 people lived in 7 houses. Of recent times the gatehouse, built around 1900, was run as a pottery by an artist and his wife, while their neighbours, a magnanimous, homely couple, provided delicious cream teas.

Although difficult of access, Culbone can be reached on foot from either the coastal footpath at Silcombe ~nearly a mile ~ or from Porlock Weir, a 40-minute woodland trek along a 'precipitous' packhorse path.

The tiny church at Culbone in its wooded setting ▶

Porlock Weir

A natural harbour, a busy port in days gone by,
　Now given way to leisure craft that drift beneath the sky,
Hotels but two, a shop or more, amenities are few,
　But patronage is plentiful with tourists out to view.

In former times a busy fishing and shipping harbour importing cargoes of limestone and Australian wool and exporting livestock and bark for tanning. Porlock Weir today is a popular spot for holiday-makers who flock to enjoy the unique beauty of its 'end of the line' setting, offering fishing and yachting as more leisurely pursuits. This tiny one-time port, sheltered by Worthy Wood and looking across to Hurlstone Point, was a natural creation when in the middle ages the sea receded further up coast, the quay, wall, and lock gates being built in the last century.

The only way out, other than retracing the route to Porlock, is to take the toll road up past Worthy, the old manor house, 'through' the attractive thatched toll cottage, and continue climbing until it joins the main A39 at a wayside inn. For those who like walking, there is a cliffside track from Porlock Weir that climbs to the remote settlement of Culbone, a 40-minute trek of some endurance, but worth the effort, culminating in seeing one of the smallest complete parish churches in England. And to bide awhile in the densely foliaged Culbone Woods where many a human drama has been played out over the centuries.

From documentation uncovered it appears that John Knight, in 1826, proposed to construct a railway from Simonsbath to Porlock Weir for lime-hauling and the transport of iron ore, the plans to include land at Porlock Weir for the building of limekilns, wharves, warehouses, and cottages for labourers, but the scheme proved too expensive and was abandoned. Later, an aerial ropeway was proposed, the ropeway to be capable of carrying 40 tons per hour at a speed of 130 yards a minute. This project also foundered as unaffordable.

Scene at Porlock Weir ▶

Porlock

The switchback road that is Porlock Hill
Is a hair~raising route, you can depend on it,
If you need an enticement to keep you going
There's a 'purty vair' village at the end of it.

In centuries past Porlock was closer to the sea and had its own harbour, having been given its name by the Saxons ~ 'the enclosed port', but as the sea receded leaving it 2 miles inland Porlock Weir emerged 1½ miles down the coast. The town itself sits in the lap of Porlock Vale, a fertile area rich in barley farming, and noted for its abundant birdlife. Entry from snaking Porlock Hill with its 1 in 4 gradient presents a difficult negotiation. The picturesque architecture of thatched and slate~roofed houses backing on to the narrow streets, and rows of cottagey shops, gives it an old~world appeal which is popular with visitors. The poet~laureate Robert Southey, who composed a sonnet in the parlour of the Ship Inn, had noted in his journal that the neighbourhood was considered 'the end of the world', inaccessible as it was to carriages on the rutted roads. Blackmore's John Ridd purchased gunpowder for his blunderbus at a Mr Pooke's shop 'The Spit and Gridiron' in his preparations against the Doones, the outlaws who had murdered his father on his way home from Porlock market. Blackmore partly wrote 'Lorna Doone' at Myrtle Cottage.

Much of the parish church of Saint Dubricius dates from the 13th century, including its truncated spire, thought to have been damaged in the great gale of 1703 but never replaced. The beautiful interior with its lancet windows contains some unique craftsmanship.

On Porlock Common are two ancient stones called the 'Whit Stones' about which legend says they were hurled in a con~ test between the devil and a giant.

In September 1940, German pilot Helmut Ackenhausen, skimming his crippled Junkers 88 low over Porlock Vale after losing a gun~ battle with Spitfires, crashed his plane on to the pebbled beach, the first enemy plane to be shot down over West Somerset.

The Ship Inn

Porlock village scene ►

THE COUNTRYMAN

Penny Housden

Bossington

Wander round the village byways,
Step inside the country scene,
Willows, walnut, maple foliage
Canopy the ancient green.

This attractive village of thatched and tiled cottages, some with round chimneys and bread ovens, and famed for its walnut trees, lies within the 12,443 acres of the Holnicote Estate. This lovely area of Somerset which embraces a variety of landscapes, was given to the National Trust in 1944 by Sir Richard Acland. In Saxon days this ancient hamlet belonged to the Abbey of Athelney.

At Bossington, the village is close to a pebbly storm beach through which the Horner Stream, which skirts the village, filters through to the sea. This barrier of pebbles, 20 feet high and 50 feet wide stretches from Hurlstone Point to Porlock Weir. It is said the walnut trees were first planted around 1800 to provide rifle stocks during the Napoleonic Wars, some of the trees also being used for gateposts, as well as for their crops of nuts.

Smuggling was inevitable along this stretch of coast, and a secret underground cache in a small field between Bossington and Porlock went undetected until 1850 when a hunted hare disappeared down a hole. After the huntsman enlarged it and sent a man down, a room was revealed, about 10 feet square and to a man's height, apparently built about a century earlier.

As a backdrop to the village, the rounded summit of Bossington Hill rises majestically to the skyline, along with the wooded heights of Selworthy Beacon, rich with the colours of the seasons. E.W. Hendy, the naturalist and writer, lived in Bossington Lane for many years.

Bossington is a good starting place for walks; one is signposted to Hurlstone Point, and the South West Coast Path passes through the village.

View of the village to Bossington Hill ▶

Penny Housden

Lynch

In a valley sheltered by rounded hills
 This small community applies its skills,
A country house lets accommodation,
 A farm park thrives on recommendation,
Flowers unfurl with a consummate ease
 A-trailing their scents on the summer breeze.

Not far from neighbouring Bossington, on the road to Allerford, the small hamlet of Lynch with its pinkly warm sandstone buildings shelters in a combe that allows a profusion of flowers to bloom late into the year. It is quite possible that the name Lynch derives from 'lynchet' which, according to the dictionary, is a ridge or ledge formed by prehistoric ploughing on slopes.

The bridge over the Aller Water leads to Lynch Country House where holiday apartments can be rented and horse riding is available. A side lane reveals attractive thatched cottages.

Opposite the stream is the chapel~of~ease, the daughter~church of Selworthy, but the dedication is unknown. It is thought to have been built around 1520 as the chapel of the manor of Bossington which belonged to Athelney Abbey from AD 920 until the dissolution of the monasteries when it was used as a barn, but was then restored by Sir Thomas Dyke Acland in 1885.

In the glass of the east window, most of which had to be re~built, can be seen the abbey seal (founded by King Alfred in 878), King Alfred's arms, the arms of the holders of the manor, with the arms of the diocese of Bath and Wells beneath the mitre. Eleven of the original bosses remain in the ancient waggon roof. In 1930 another restoration took place when the organ gallery was built with wood taken from the old box pews in the parish church.

Close to the chapel is a farm park.

Bridge over the Aller Water ▶

Penny Hausden

Allerford

An idyllic scene that lingers in the past
  When burdened beast, slung heavy with its load,
Traversed the fords on bridges scarce their width
  Recalling times of transport's only mode.

Taking its name from the gentle Aller Water which passes through this Domesday village, Allerford, in the parish of Selworthy, is both popular and famous for its quaint packhorse bridge straddling the ford beside the picturesque red-stoned cottage, dormer-windowed, with its square and round sandstone chimneys and protruding bread oven. Beyond the two-arched bridge, cobble-stoned and 4 feet wide, a well-worn track climbs steeply up the wooded slopes towards Selworthy and the mother church. On the other side of the ford the Packhorse Inn is aptly named and offers accommodation to holiday-makers.

There are many interesting dwellings of great age. The old schoolhouse, which celebrated its 150th birthday in 1972 is now a rural life museum, but used to double up as the village hall for special social occasions. The blacksmith's premises are still intact although shoeing is carried out elsewhere. Many trades and shops have disappeared: bootmaker, fishmonger, market gardener, laundry service, etc.

General repairs were carried out by the carpenter from Brandish Street a few hundred yards distant where the group of appealing cottages and farmsteads are still retained in their original setting amidst fields where the Aller passes under two small bridges, and where A.R. Quinton painted one of his renowned watercolours. The lane thence meets up with the A39 main road.

Across the road, in a sheltered nook, Piles Mill with its 10-foot diameter over-shot water-wheel, and housing 2 pairs of mill stones, is driven by a long leat off the Aller. It is owned by the National Trust and now serves as a small rural museum. A few yards further downstream is a medieval dipping well, set back from the stream to enable water to filter through, so purifying it for drinking.

The Packhorse Inn

The much-photographed house beside the packhorse bridge ▶

Penny Housden

Selworthy

A little bit special this country scene
Cottages of thatch round a sloping green,
A brook gently burbling, the wind but a sigh,
Time to reflect on the ages gone by.

This picture postcard village of thatched cottages, including a tea-garden and National Trust shop, clustered round an old-world green, is set within the Holnicote Estate (pronounced Hunnicut) which embraces 12,443 acres of varying landscape. This land was given to the National Trust in 1944 by Sir Richard Acland, the 15th baronet, in whose family it had been for 200 years.

Of architectural interest is the 14th century tithe barn in the grounds of the former rectory, in the centre of which is a blocked opening through which sheaves of corn would have been passed to the rector.

Prominent on its hill above the green in a weather-proofed coating of lime and tallow to preserve the local stone of which it is built, the parish church of All Saints can be seen as a landmark for miles around. The church tower, in the early Perpendicular style, is of the late 14th century, and the clock, some 400 years old, still keeps good time.

The interior is full of historical interest. The font is believed to be of Norman origin, the carved oak pulpit is late med- ieval and retains the hourglass by which services were timed, the altar rails are of Queen Anne's time. Above the altar the leather-embossed reredos (picture of angels) is attrib- uted to Philip Burgess of West Porlock in 1900, and a well- designed gallery at the west end of the nave was occupied by musicians from 1750.

Many walks have been created in the high-rising Selworthy Woods, at the top of which is a memorial hut commemorating the 10th baronet Sir Thomas Dyke Acland (1787-1871), in- scribed with quotations by Keble and Heber.

Cottage called 'Lorna Doone' ▶

46

Minehead

Where tall ships and seafarers plied trade across the sea,
And weather-beaten fishermen spread nets out on the quay,
Those times are past, now pleasure cruisers ride the ocean waves
To serve the tripper's longing for adventure that he craves,
The romance of those far-off days is easy brought to fore
By quayside rail ~ in quiet mood ~ salt breezes ~ shingled shore.

Although just outside the northern boundary of the Exmoor National Park to the east, Minehead never~ theless has always in the past played a vital part in the import and export of Exmoor's products. Once a seaport of considerable importance, and famous for its herring fisheries, the environs of today embrace a large seaside resort catering mainly for tourists and providing the usual holiday facilities, including a theatre on the seafront. When the tide recedes it sometimes exposes the stumps of a long lost forest. The West Somerset steam railway runs from Minehead along the coast to Watchet.

Situated round an expansive bay at the mouth of the Bristol Channel, Minehead divides into three distinct sections, namely, Higher Town, Lower Town, and Quay Town, the latter being the oldest part with its row of the original fishermen's cottages flanking the old harbour which dates back to 1616. Of interest on the quay is the fishermen's chapel of St. Peter which is unique in that it forms part of licensed premises. It was once a salt store built in 1630 for the poor by Robert Quirck, a Minehead mariner, and it is only in recent times that services have been held there. At Quay West a pier 700 feet long that was built in 1901 was dismantled in 1940 against poss~ ible invasion. A legacy of the war is the retained 6-mile mili~ tary road over the town's North Hill to Selworthy Beacon, 1,013 feet, ~ 'the window on Exmoor'.

At Lower Town, in 1630, Robert Quirck also donated to the aged of the town the row of almshouses in Market House Lane built on the site of the old market place. The area expanded to accomm~ odate the influx of visitors each year and in the Avenue and the Parade shops, boarding houses and hotels predominate.

In the lofty Higher Town, the 14th century church of St. Michael overlooks the picturesque church steps cottages.

The Quayside

View towards North Hill

48

Penny Housden

49

EASTERN EXMOOR

Eastern Exmoor

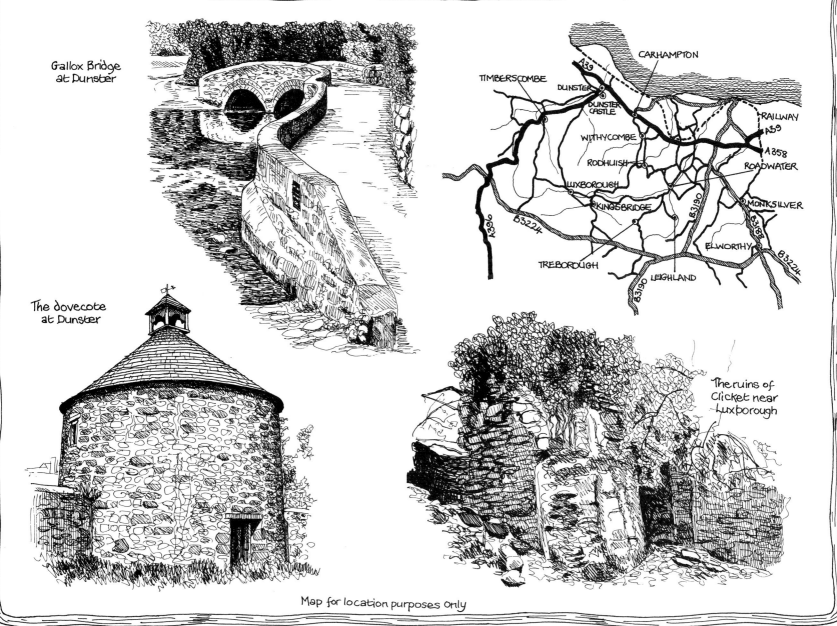

Gallox Bridge at Dunster

The dovecote at Dunster

The ruins of Clicket near Luxborough

TIMBERSCOMBE
CARHAMPTON
DUNSTER
DUNSTER CASTLE
A39
RAILWAY
A39
A358
WITHYCOMBE
RODHUISH
ROADWATER
LUXBOROUGH
B3190
MONKSILVER
KINGSBRIDGE
B3224
B3190
B396
TREBOROUGH
ELWORTHY
B3224
LEIGHLAND

Map for location purposes only

51

Dunster

Down ancient cobble-stones I tread
Trailing history's unbroken thread,
In glorious compass this 'Pearl of the West'
Captures the essence of all that is best.

One of the finest medieval villages in the West Country, entrenched in history, Dunster is in an attractive setting, overlooked at the north end by the 18th century landmark, Conygar Tower, and to the south on high ground by the dominant Norman castle, built in 1070.

Rows of quaint uneven cottages and shops of many ages line both sides of the wide High Street where once a collection of buildings, called the Shambles, ran down the middle of the road, but which were pulled down in 1825. Buildings of interest are the octagonal-structured Tudor Yarn Market built in 1609, famous for its cloths known as 'Dunsters' when the wool trade flourished; the ivy-mantled Luttrell Arms Hotel with its arched doorway, bought by the Luttrell family in 1499 and pre-viously called the Ship Inn; the Nunnery, a 3-storeyed tile-hung dwelling, a gift from Sir Hugh Pero of Oaktrow to Cleeve Abbey in 1346, although never a religious establishment, and the medieval dovecote.

The church, dedicated to St. George, is built of red sandstone and has a history dating from Norman times. The impressive tower carries a peal of 8 bells, and the magnificent rood screen of 14 openings supports a gallery. It was once divided into two churches ~ a Bene-dictine priory, and the parish church, but became one church after the monasteries were dissolved by Henry VIII.

The packhorse bridge over the Avill, called Doddebridge in the 14th century, was renamed Gallox Bridge in the reign of Henry VIII because of the gallows erected on the above hill, and the picturesque Domesday mill, now in working order after full restoration in recent years, produces flour for breadmaking. Above the village there are lovely walks on Grabbist Hill.

High Street and the Tudor yarn market ▶

Penny Housden

Dunster Castle

Eternal as time in a story-book setting
  The 'Castelle of Dunnestorre' holds to its hill,
It's saga unfolding in History's pages,
  A rattle of bones as the stories spill.

From the year 1070 when it was first built until 1974 when it passed into the hands of the National Trust, the castle on its 'tor' ~ surrounded by magnificent scenery ~ has been in the ownership of only two families, the de Mohuns and the Luttrells, the latter taking over in 1376.

Of the original Norman structure built by the first de Mohun only a tower to the north flanked by a battlemented wall remains intact, but succeeding de Mohuns added and enlarged over the centuries, including a gatehouse with an iron~studded oak door in 1220, still in fine condition. At that time an itin~erary of the buildings in use on the tor listed a kitchen and bakehouse, pantry, a hall with buttery, a Knight's hall, a chapel, 3 towers and a prison. A second gatehouse was built in 1409 known today as the Gateway.

A formidable 12th-century keep on the summit which towered above the castle was one of the casualties of the Civil War when Cromwell ordered its destruction. During restorations in 1869 the skeleton of a man 7 feet in height and locked in iron fetters was found buried in the wall of the Guardhouse.

The gatehouse

It was in 1680, when Francis Luttrell married the heiress Mary Tregonwell of Milton Abbas in Dorset and they adopted an extravagant lifestyle, that the ornate ceilings and splendidly~carved staircase depicting stag and fox~hunting scenes were installed.

Between 1867 and 1872 the castle was reconstructed by George Fownes Luttrell in an endeavour to make the living quarters more comfortable.

The castle is open to visitors from April to October.

Dunster Castle ▶

Carhampton

Old paintings show a long and dusty street
  Where children play and friendly neighbours meet,
Today, that pace of living's long since gone
As endless traffic hurtles swiftly on.

The village of Carhampton, 3 miles east of Minehead, made famous by the 'Carhampton Hundreds' as recorded in the Domesday Book, has in past history been known by many variations of its name. The 6th-century 'Carrum' from Saint Carantoc the Celtic saint from Wales, 'Carr' (the low-lying land on Carhampton beach is known as Carr Moor), 'Catum' a diminutive of Carentokes Town mentioned by Lelant the antiquary of Henry VIII, and 'Karenton' which was referred to in a document of 1180. It has legends of King Arthur and the dragons (Viking ships).

Due to a revision of parish boundaries in 1954 Carhampton relinquished all its detached areas, duly annexed by Dunster, Timberscombe and Withycombe. The long village street of shops, houses and inns straggles along the route between Williton and Minehead, and it was in this area that Turner sat and painted his memorable picture of Dunster Castle.

The church of St. John the Baptist was fully restored in 1862~70, having its origins in the 14th century, and was first registered to baptisms, marriages and burials in 1634. It has a 15th-century rood screen repainted in re~ cent times to a faithful and colourful representation of that time, as are preserved the waggon roof of the same period, and a Perpendicular aisle 6~bay arcade. There are 2 piscinas, an 18th-century pulpit, an ancient iron~banded wooden chest, and a peal of 6 bells. The one beautiful stained-glass window depicts the Last Supper.

Track to Blue Anchor Bay

The custom of apple~wassailing is observed annually on 17th January. From Carhampton's main street there is a sign~ posted track to Blue Anchor Bay, crossing over the West Somerset railway line.

Thatched residence fore-fronting the church of St. John the Baptist ▶

56

Withycombe

A village street of rare delight
  Where tribulations take to flight,
Away from noise and city stress
  The air is one of peacefulness.

Pleasantly situated between Rodhuish and Carhampton well away from the mainstream traffic, the row of pink, white and cream~coloured cottages with names like 'Squirrels' and 'Laurel' straggles down the hill beside its little stream which makes a ford at the dip by Rattle Row, and which once powered the mill. A 'cottage stores' incorporating a post office, its white walls brightened by hanging flower baskets, serves the needs of the community. A sense of peace pervades the village which lies at the entrance to a deep valley of rounded hills and sturdy oakwoods, and leads to the track up Withycombe Hill.

High on its grassy mound the parish church of St. Nicholas with its roughcast exterior is of 13th cen~ tury origin. The embattled tower is 40 feet high with small one~light bell openings, and in 1903 and again in 1936 it underwent major repairs, when the 4 bells were realigned.

Facing the main door is the effigy of an unknown lady with a lacy head cover on the lid of a stone coffin dated 1300 which was opened in 1913 and found empty. But it is believed to be that of Lucy de Meriet (wife of Thomas of Tymworth), who owned the manor of Withycombe, now called Sandhill. Another effigy dated 1290 half hidden in the south wall is thought to be of Thomas of Tymworth who was Constable of Taunton Castle. It is unusual in that his hat is one of the earliest to appear on a monument of this sort in England. Both effigies are carved in Somerset Ham Hill stone.

The greatest treasure in the church is the rood screen, car~ ved around 1500, said to be one of 7 fan~vaulted rood screens made at Dunster by Flemish craftsmen.

Cottages at Withycombe ▶

Penny Housden

Rodhuish

Down deepset lanes of ancient tread
  Where miscreants could lose their head,
When prevalent the parson's saw
  And village folk would pray the more,
It's said those brimstone days of old
  Led lost sheep back into the fold.

A pretty village of quiet lanes and sandstone barns that has a faint air of righteousness and quaint re~ spectability, no doubt engendered by its history of gospelling parsons and the sight of the Felon's Oak on its traditional patch of green. The oak tree, as its name implies, was used as a gallows to hang the criminal element in its midst, and one can only imagine the gruesome pageant of the execution. A young sapling has now taken its place. The name 'Rodhuish' means 'dwelling place of the radman or judge'.

There is a small white~washed chapel to St. Bartholomew in which the chalice and silver were given by a Richard Escott who was the local benefactor in the 18th century. A farm and woods in the vicinity bear the Escott name. Also, in a grassy enclosure, is a little tin tabernacle, built around 1899, which is held in affection by the villagers as a little of the revered past to cling on to.

Most areas contain a mystery and the one here concerns a German aristocrat, Count Conrad von Hochberg, who lived at Croydon Hall, a secluded mansion close by, and who disappeared 7 days be~ fore the declaration of war between England and Germany on 4 August 1914. He was a cousin of the Kaiser and had been resident there since 1907, known to love England and its people, and a generous benefactor. The sinister quest~ ion arose ~ had he been spying for the Fatherland? Rumours of espionage and wild stories abounded. As late as 24 July the Count had given a garden party for his friends. After~ wards, some reckoned it had been his way of saying goodbye.

The mystery of his disappearance was never discovered. To~ day, Croydon Hall is a school for maladjusted children.

St. Bartholomew

A Rodhuish lane ►

Roadwater

Charming little backwaters
Down lanes of narrow span
Give a village 'something more'
Than just a one~street scan.

In a valley running north from the Brendon Hills Roadwater village, in the parish of Old Cleeve, is a long stretch of road with pretty houses, post office and general store, the church of St. Luke's, and a chapel. A narrow byway leads to a pink sandstone cottage with latticed windows and ivy~clad walls that was once the village bakery. The village hall was given to Roadwater by the family of artist Rachel Reckitt of Golsoncott.

Streams of the Washford River draining from the Brendon Hills fan out on the upper reaches of the Road~water valley, one branch winding round the deep bowl at Comberow, another winding with the valley through Druid's Combe towards Kingsbridge. These two main branches of the Washford join together on the edge of Roadwater behind a thatched cottage called 'Watersmeet', passing through the village un~seen behind the houses to emerge near Manor Mill. This is a sturdy stone building with a projecting roof that sheltered the outside sack hoist, but the wheel has now gone.

One of the biggest streams runs down parallel with the old disused West Somerset Mineral Railway incline along its first 1,100 yards at a gradient of 1 in 4. This used to carry the iron ore from the mines on the Brendons to the port of Watchet via Roadwater to Comberow in 1857.

The Reverend Lewis Court, an organist at Roadwater Chapel who published a collection of carols, wrote about Thomas Slade, the blacksmith, who learned to play the cello and then formed a band of Roadwater musicians. At Christmas time they would go round the houses playing and singing the carols. It was the last Bible Christian chapel to be built (in 1907) in England.

The erstwhile village bakery, now a private house ▶

Penny Housden

63

Monksilver

Enchanting cottage homes of sweet appeal
  Born to the peace and quiet of a country lane,
Face now the speeding wheels of time's progress,
  Caught in the frenzied twentieth-century bane.

Despite its position directly on to the Wiveliscombe to Watchet road on the eastern boundary, Monksilver is a village of quaint cottages and old~world charm that conjures up the past. The Notley Arms with its spacious 19th-century converted coach-house which belonged to a former inn dominates the main street; the old schoolhouse, tucked up a side road and now residential, retains its old bell; the old post office, no longer operating, shows a date of 1609.

Set back on rising ground the church of All Saints contains a rare eagle lectern, carved bench ends and an ornate wooden font cover. In the churchyard can be seen graves of the Notley family who once owned nearby Combe Sydenham, a Tudor manor house, now open to the public. Here a cannon ball is on display. Legend has it that heiress Elizabeth Sydenham, in the absence of Sir Francis Drake to whom she was betrothed, was about to marry another when a cannon ball came out of the skies and landed on the train of her gown, which sent her scurrying home to await Drake's return.

The old schoolhouse

In 1773, a mile north of Monksilver in the hamlet of Woodford, an elderly mother, Mrs Elizabeth Conibeer, and her two middle-aged daughters Ann and Sarah, were found brutally murdered. Their tomb at Monksilver bears the warning:
  'Inhuman Wretch, who e'er thou art
  That didst commit this hainous Crime,
  Repent, before thou dost depart
  To meet the Awfull Judge Divine.'

To the west in a park-like setting is Nettlecombe Court, an impressive Elizabethan mansion on the Trevelyan Estate, now run as a centre for field studies. The tree~shrouded church next to it is full of the relics of past ages.

Cottages fronting the village street ▶

Elworthy

A place where one can wish awhile
In solitude with peace prevailing,
What sweeter dreams than country style
For shaking off whatever's ailing.

An enchanting little backwater set within the middle-eastern perimeter of the National Park and the extreme edge of the Brendon Hills. Two miles south of Monksilver, this small settlement contains but few cottages and farms and is cradled amidst fields and pastures on gently rising ground. Its name means 'old village', the manor having been given to William de Mohun of Dunster by the Conqueror.

Along a deep hedged lane and higher up in a leafy nook the stone church of St. Martin's with its castellated tower dates back to the 13th century and is presently the subject of restoration. In the small interior it has an interesting lancet window in the nave portraying two traditional figures, one with the symbolic eagle, the other with the sacrificial lamb, and on the south wall hangs a framed picture of Alexander Morley, Rector 1717~1731. A handsome rose and thistle decorated screen bears the inscription 'Lord prepare our Arts to Pray. Anno 1632'. It is said of the chancel, which is a little askew, that it typifies the position of the Saviour's head when on the cross.

Although there are tumuli in the vicinity, about a mile south~west of the hamlet at a height of around 1,200 feet an Iron Age hill fort is mistakenly called Elworthy Barrows, and a little to the south~east, on Willett Hill, is a ruined tower said to have been built with a stone staircase and a 'lookout', at the request of a female personage for her pleasure of surveying the surrounding terrain.

St. Martin's Church

View across the meadow ▶

Penny Housden

Leighland

On wooded slopes the small stone church
Stands valiant and true,
While crinolines of foliage
Shade cottages from view.

Leighland is a small parish off the beaten track between Roadwater and Ralegh's Cross, and was created only as recently as 1865 when the present parish church of St. Giles was built to replace an ancient chapel. An extract from 'Memorials of the Cistercian Abbey of St. Mary, Old Cleeve, and the Benedictine Priory Church of St. George, Dunster' states 'On May 28th 1320, a Vicarage was constituted by the Bishop of Bath and Wells whereby the perpetual Vicar had a house and curtilage and all oblations and profits accruing to the Church of Cleeve and the Chapel of St. Giles of Leigh with the tithe of mills, wool, lambs, kids, calves, pigs, geese, pidgeons, eggs, honey, flax, cheese, butter, apples, burials & Requiem and all other tithes with the herbage of the Parish Cemetry'.

At the west end of the church a panel depicting St. Giles in his abbot's habit and a deer at his feet (associated with his supernatural agency) was painted by Rachel Reckitt of Golsoncott.

Just to the north is Stamborough Farm, once the home of the artist John William North who died in 1924, and whose sketches and paintings portrayed scenes of the area including 'Exmoor Ponies' and 'Landscape with Chapel'.

Less than a mile south-west stands the building of Leigh Barton with its Ham stone porch and barns, the home of the Poyntz family in the 16th century. A Douai priest, Dom Philip Powel was retained as their chaplain and had his own chapel there. As a Royalist during the Civil War Powel was captured by the enemy and sentenced to death. A service in his memory on the June anniversary of his execution is commemorated by the rector and parishioners of Old Cleeve.

Church of St. Giles ▶

68

Treborough

There was a time when peasantry worked fingers to the bone,
Hacking out a living, be it iron, or slate, or stone,
Diligent providers of a family, home and hearth,
Following age~old principles along the righteous path.

High and lonely in its isolated position bordering the roadside, open to the wintry gales blowing off the Brendon Hills, this is a village of few houses with no shopping amenity.

Treborough was once famous for its slate quarries which were worked for many a century, providing the roofs for most of the houses on Exmoor over their walls of Brendon stone. Then, there were many more cottages to house the workers, and it was a busy little place up until 1938 when the industry came to a halt. Also living here were over a hundred families of miners who worked the iron mine at nearby Ralegh's Cross, but this had closed down well before 1900.

On Sundays they worshipped at the ancient church of St. Peter, purported to be the third highest church in all southern England, where the register shows that the first induction of a rector was in 1322, although there appears to have been an earlier church. Of Perpendicular style with a pyramid roof to the tower, it was extensively reconstructed in the mid~19th century, and has a 500~year~old font, and a medieval piscina on a pedestal in the north wall of the chancel. The wooden pulpit is said to be older than the Reformation.

In one corner of the churchyard there is a reinterred prehistoric skeleton. This was discovered in Langridge Wood in 1820 by workers who, digging for stone for road repairs, uncovered a slate~lined grave under a small round barrow dating from between 1500 and 2000 B.C. It is the only known slate~lined grave visible on Exmoor and lies about 1,200 yards north-north-east of the church.

The area around Treborough is designated a conservation area.

Church of St. Peter in its lonely setting ▶

70

Penny Housden

Luxborough

The stone church stands upon its hallowed ground
Overlooking fields of lush domain,
Slow grazing sheep, the while put out to pasture,
Depict a scene in true pastoral vein.

Luxborough, in its combe amidst the Brendon Hills, is one of three hamlets overrunning one another, the other two being Churchtown to its immediate north~west and Kingsbridge to its south~east, and comprises a scattering of houses and farms that have presented an unchanging scene down the ages. It included a one~time inn and a schoolhouse that served children from outlying farms and hamlets, but which have now been converted to houses.

Churchtown is the hilltop purlieu of the red sandstone church of St. Mary's with its slate~roofed saddle~backed tower which stands in regal surveillance over the parish and surrounding area. Between 1142 and 1166 Robert of Luxborough, Lord of the Manor, assigned the church to Bruton Priory founded by William de Mohun, Lord of Dunster, in 1142. In 1175 William de Mohun's son granted the church in his manor of Cutcombe to the same foundation, thus linking the churches of Luxborough and Cutcombe, an arrangement that outlasted the dissolution of Bruton Priory in 1539, and remains to this day, one vicar serving both churches.

St. Mary's
Church

The views from Luxborough are refreshing to the eye, the green verdure of Croydon Hill to the north, the rich foliage of Slowley Wood to the east, though much is planted to conifers.

North of Luxborough a deepcut lane at Nurcott Farm leads to the derelict village of Clicket a mile on; rough going in wet weather. Now in ruins and hidden in an overgrown thicket of woods, with trees growing out of the interiors, and fallen boughs barricading the ground, it is difficult to identify the purpose of any particular dwelling. The dark canopy of leaves shading out light creates a sinister note, while below, a stream, choked by weeds and rotting branches, struggles on its way through the valley.

Aspect of the village ►

72

Kingsbridge

A rustic air of permanence unfurled,
 Unchanging in an ever-changing world,
'Neath sheltered eaves of slate and golden thatch
 Nest migrant birds, their families to hatch.

From Churchtown and Luxborough the road continues east into Kingsbridge at the foot of the parish where the white-coated Royal Oak Inn welcomes the traveller alongside attractive stone cottages, thatched and tiled, a shop and post office and a chapel.

From its headwaters high up on the Brendon Hills and trickling down from the grassy slopes of Lype Hill at 1,390 feet, Kennisham Hill, and the woods of Langham Hill, one of the main waters of the Washford River runs into Kingsbridge, flowing by the Methodist chapel, past New Mills, now converted to a field study centre, and on beside the road through a densely wooded valley towards Roadwater where it meets up with the eastern branch of the Washford.

To the south, where the streams meet up below Chargot House ~ built by Sir Thomas Lethbridge in 1827, and acquired by the Malet family in 1926 ~ they serve to feed a series of fishponds that enhance the parklands of copper beeches and rhododendron walkways. Chargot House was, in 1890, one of the first private houses to have its own electric light. Sir Edward Malet, in 1979, wrote about local life in the 1920s and 30s and the characters of the village at that time.

In the 20s there used to be a pleasant coach trip from Chargot to Brendon Hill along a grassy track lined with stands of beech and oak and abounding in wild life, but this has long since vanished beneath a metalled road along with nature's abundance.

There has also been a short history of the mining of iron ore within the parish and outside but few signs remain of that era.

The Royal Oak in the centre of the village ►

The Royal Oak of Luxborough
Free House

The Royal Oak of Luxborough

Penny Housden

'75

Timberscombe

The grand old church on rising ground
Looks down upon its flock,
In ageless span the village stands
Enduring as a rock.

'The Wooded Combe'. Thus wrote Collinson, the historian, to describe the lovely country of rich woods and lush meadows in which the parish of Timberscombe has its home. Grey-slated, tiled and thatched cottages mingle in a picturesque cluster at the foot of its place of worship, with village inns, a school, post office and stores to complete the picture.

Rising steps lead up to the red sandstone church dedicated to Saint Petrock who was one of the famous missionaries from Wales to the West Country where he founded many churches. Most of the present structure is of 15th century date, the tower being rebuilt in 1705 by the village bene~ factor Richard Elsworth. The chancel and north doorway are about 1450 and the south aisle was added in the 16th century, its east window still retaining fragments of ancient glass. The interior houses many interesting features ~ a fan-vaulted screen about 1500, piscinas for two altars, a 15th-century font, a 17th-century pulpit. Both the lectern and nave were designed and crafted locally. Above the south door~ way is a mural painting of King David believed to date from the Reformation but which was only dis~ covered in 1955. There is a peal of 8 bells.

The bubbly little streams of the River Avill that drain off Dun~ kery and the Brendons meet up on the level at Timberscombe and then course on through the Avill Vale towards Dunster and the sea. Where the Avill flows under the narrow valley road known as Draper's Way, and as far as Pitt Bridge, the banks and woods are carpeted in February and March with thousands of snowdrops, called locally Snowdrop Valley. The National Park Authority have sign~posted walks through the woods but the gathering of snowdrops is strictly prohibited.

Timberscombe village centre ►

Penny Housden

CENTRAL EXMOOR

Central Exmoor

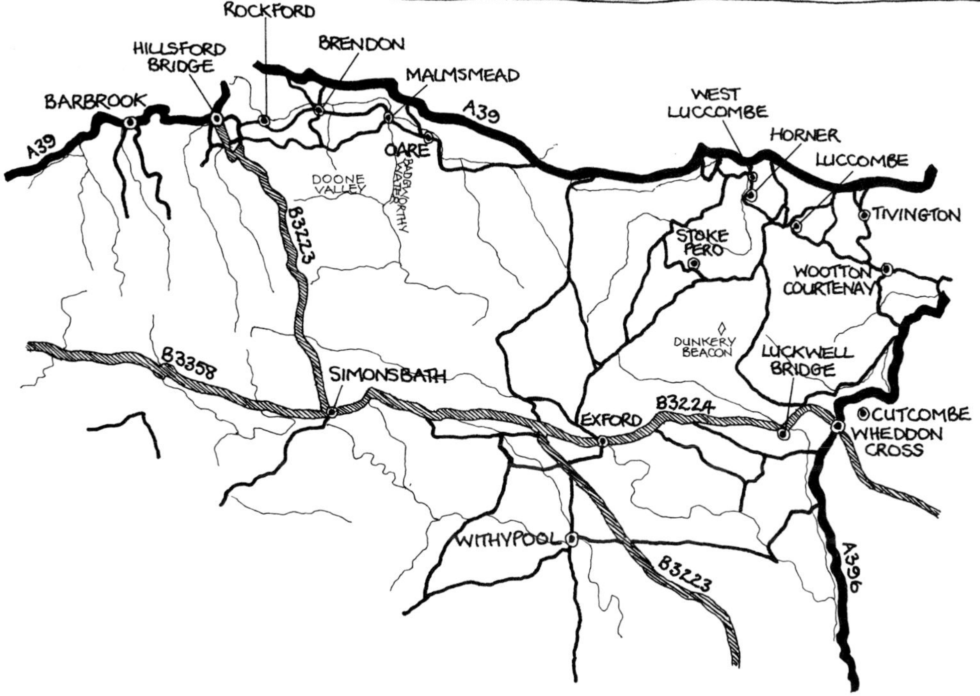
ROCKFORD
HILLSFORD BRIDGE
BRENDON
MALMSMEAD
BARBROOK
A39
A39
OARE
DOONE VALLEY
BADGWORTHY WATER
B3223
WEST LUCCOMBE
HORNER
LUCCOMBE
TIVINGTON
STOKE PERO
WOOTTON COURTENAY
DUNKERY BEACON
LUCKWELL BRIDGE
B3358
SIMONSBATH
EXFORD
B3224
CUTCOMBE
WHEDDON CROSS
WITHYPOOL
B3223
A396

Robber's Bridge

Lank Combe (Doone Valley)

Dunkery Beacon

Map for location purposes only

Cutcombe

Look out upon the beauty~laden hills,
  Fulfilling nature's role of bounteousness,
It can but lift the heart when it instils
  An inner radiance of joyousness.

A pretty little village bounded by the richness of rounded purple hills, deep combes, and enchanting woodlands, and in the distance the lofty height of Dunkery Beacon about which Blackmore had John Fry say 'the haighest place of Hexmoor', which it is at 1,705 feet above sea-level. Cutcombe and its woods were once part of the old Royal Forest of Exmoor until this area's disafforestation in 1300, but the red deer can still be seen in Cutcombe woods.

The ancient parish church of Saint John the Evangelist is typical of the style prevalent in the hill districts of Exmoor and its position on rising ground overlooks magnificent countryside. Although an earlier church appears to have occupied the site after the Norman Conquest, little remains of that period. It is believed the north aisle was added during the 14th century, the tower during the 15th. The roof over the nave with its finely carved bosses was also added at this time. The south aisle and chapel, together with the south arcade, were added during the 19th. Most of the furnishings belong to this period. The reredos is a representation of the Last Supper.

Church of Saint John
the Evangelist

Cutcombe, for all its remoteness, was ravaged by the Black Death in the winter of 1348~9 when there were three rectors in quick succession. The parish clerk also perished.

A later incumbent, the Rev. Arthur Courtenay Jenoure, became nationally famous through his outspokenness from the pulpit over a missing local girl, Mollie Phillips, whose dead body was found fifteen months later in a bog on Codsend Moor in mysterious circumstances, and whom he believed had been murdered. It was a case that was never satisfactorily concluded.

Village cottages ►

Penny Housden

Wheddon Cross

'Rest and be Thankful' an inn implores
Across the road from the village stores,
The schoolhouse sleeps in the noon~day sun,
Young folk's holidays have just begun.

Situated 1,000 feet above sea-level at the highest point between Dulverton and Dunster, the hamlet of Wheddon Cross in the parish of Cutcombe overlooks the valleys of the rivers Avill and Quarme, and has views towards the higher Dunkery Beacon. Crossroads intersecting the hamlet keep the traveller wary, whether driving or walking, and care should be taken. On one corner the 16th-century coaching inn called 'The Rest and be Thankful Inn' has a large car park and offers real ale and a variety of amenities. Almost opposite there is a post office/general stores and newsagents, and thatched houses called 'Normans Cottages', adjacent to which is the schoolhouse and a memorial cross.

The area abounds in ghost stories, more so at Wheddon Cross than on any other part of the moor, but none more credible than the phantom hearse that haunts Cutcombe Hill into the village. On a dark night, the death~coach has been witnessed on a number of occasions, enough to send a chill down the recipient's spine. On a night in 1929 two girls leaving the village 'hop' started off down the long, winding road that was once the route of the coach and four. What they saw was recorded in several newspapers, they having turned tail and run back in terror to the safety of the dance hall.

The war memorial

The story most publicised was of a Winsford farmer who, at a hostelry in the late 19th century, having heard about the phantom hearse, boasted that he would drive his gig down Cutcombe Hill that night. Later his terrified horse was seen galloping along without him, bathed in sweat. A search party eventually found him lying face down on Cutcombe Hill, though not a word were they able to get out of him, not then, nor ever.

Normans Cottages adjacent to the school ▶

Penny Housden

Luckwell Bridge

Time passes in a changing world
  Where once the smithy nailed the shoe,
Under the bridge in timeless style
  The river flows unchanged and true.

This small farming community of a few cottages and a red sandstone bridge just off the road between Exford and Wheddon Cross is easily missed by visitors. The bridge spans the River Quarme, a fair~sized stream, which has its source on the rough grassland of Hoar Moor between Exford Common and Codsend Moor 1500 feet up. The name is a derivation of St. Luke's Well, a one~time healing well, now covered by a heap of stones in a nearby field. Before the building of the Dunster to Dulverton turnpike road in the early 19th century, Luckwell Bridge was an important junction of 5 roads with a couple of mills, an inn, a smithy, and a chapel. The chapel beside the bridge, built in 1884, has been converted to living accommodation, an earlier~built chapel being incorporated into Steppes Cottage. One of the old tracks, now a grass~ covered bridlepath, can still be followed along the right bank to Wheddon Cross.

Higher on the main road there are a few houses, one called The Old Inn, another called The Old Forge, re~ miniscent of the old coaching days. When the population was a goodly number there were more cott~ ages and some shops, and the usual coterie of craftsmen. Today it is a quiet backwater surrounded by fields of sheep and a few ponies in a pretty woodland setting.

In the vicinity is West Mill, partly converted to domestic use, but with a lot of the mill machinery remaining in~ tact. This includes a wire and brush machine used for grading the meal after it was ground, a job once executed by a hand~held sieve known as a 'temse'. A fast~ working miller would be said to be 'setting the temse on fire'. From thus came the connotation 'Setting the Thames on fire'. Attached to the mill is a disused smithy.

Looking towards the bridge ▶

Exford

Dwellings grouped round a spacious green,
  The river running wide and clean,
Hunting, fishing, trekking, hiking,
  All things geared to the tourist's liking.

Geographically the centre of the National Park, Exford's claim to be the sporting capital of Exmoor had its beginnings when Fenwick Bissett, Master of the Devon and Somerset Staghounds from 1855~1881, built the stables and kennels at Exford in 1875, thereby establishing it as an important hunting and riding mecca, providing employment for 12 per cent of the population.

Add to the village what some people consider to be the loveliest river on Exmoor, and indeed in the West Country, the Exe flowing through its confines, and it can be seen to have a lot going for it in the way of tourism from which it derives its main income, backed up by sheep-farming.

The source of the Exe lies 1,450 feet up on the eastern edge of the windswept wilderness called The Chains. By the time it reaches Exford it is a full twenty feet across as it runs under the three~arched bridge in front of the White Horse Inn, an attractive ivy~clad building. Here, during the flood disaster of 1952 water rose to a height of five feet in the inn, tearing off doors and windows, and sweeping away the building where 22 horses were stabled.

Detached from the village up a steep incline, close to a pre~historic trackway, is the church dedicated to St. Salvyn, a Celtic missionary, who is delineated in a stained glass window. Although of ancient foundation, the church has been built more than once, the oldest part being the tower of mid-15th century date. The rood screen, a fine piece of craftmanship dating from the 15th century, was a gift, and once belonged to the old church of St. Audries near Watchet. In the churchyard, a base and shaft are all that is left of the cross, believed to have been destroyed by Cromwell's men.

The White Horse Inn beside the bridge ▶

Withypool

A precious jewel, set at the heart of the moor,
Encircled by a ring of heathered moorland hills,
Linked to the past by hardy forebears' earthly span
They so endured, and paved the way for future man.

Immured in the very heart of the moor and encompassed by acres of moorland, Withypool is one of the oldest settlements associated as it is with the Royal Forest environs over the thousand years of its existence as a Royal hunting and game preserve.

Together with Hawkridge the two villages held between them a total of 52 Free Suitors, and were small farmers who were permitted to hold land, free of charge, within the Royal Forest with certain grazing rights and privileges like turf cutting and fishing consent in return for executing duties under Forest laws.

Withypool today is a small but attractive village of stone and slate containing a post office, off licence, stores and garage, a chapel~of~ease dedicated to St. Andrew's, and the Royal Oak Inn where R.D. Blackmore is said to have carried out his research, and had his shirts made by the innkeeper's wife. Down by the six~arched bridge over the Barle (one of the moor's two chief rivers) are the weeping willows which gave Withypool its name, withy or withe pertaining to a willow or osier branch.

To the west, spanning the Barle, is the five~arched 16th~ century Landacre Bridge (pronounced Lannaker), a beauty spot on the common. It was here, in 'Lorna Doone', that the King's Officer, Jeremy Stickles, and a trooper, were am~ bushed by the Doone outlaws. Half-a-mile below Withypool 24 rough~hewn stepping stones form a crossing over the river but these are frequently awash.

Relics of prehistoric man can be found in the stone circle on Withypool Hill and the barrows on Withypool Common.

Withypool village and Common ▶

Penny Housden

Simonsbath

Where it all started, the history books say,
   By a family who took the moor under its sway,
Taming the land into civilised living,
   Planting beech hedges and generously giving.

It was here, in the heart of the ancient Royal Forest that the beginnings of civilisation were carved out of Exmoor by John Knight of Worcestershire who in 1818 purchased from the Crown 10,000 acres for £50,000, thereafter taking up residence with his family at Simonsbath, later acquiring more land. John Knight and his son Frederic set about agricultural experiments, building cottages for the labourers and constructing 22 miles of beech-hedged lanes for windbreaks and easy transport of equipment. The manor house he started was never completed, the walls being demolished in 1899, but he erected a wall around his estate of some 29 miles. Although Simonsbath itself is little more than a hamlet with its small church of St. Luke, built in 1856, a parsonage and a school, Exmoor as it exists today is as a result of the Knight Family's super-human endeavours.

For centuries previously the moorland had been leased out to wardens who rented summer grazing to farmers who maintained the boundaries. Simonsbath House was the first dwelling to be built in the Forest, around 1651, under the Wardenship of James Boevey, a formidable tyrant who extracted too-high fees from his tenants and was feared and hated by all.

Pinkworthy Pond, created from a damming of the Barle from off The Chains, was another of the Knight ventures. Twice the lake has been drained; the first time in 1889 revealing the missing body of Farmer Gammon of Parracombe, who in a case of unrequited love, had been heard to say 'Then I'm off to Pinkery'. The second, in 1913, in search of a William Stenner of Riscombe, near Exford, was without avail. He was found dead weeks later, not far from his own cottage.

At the junction of the White Water and the Barle stands lofty Cow Castle, the most impressive Iron Age fortress on Exmoor.

The E-shaped Simonsbath House Hotel ▶

THE SIMONSBATH HOUSE HOTEL

SIMONSBATH

Penny Housden

Barbrook

A village with a memory that never will recede
Remindful of the suffering that it knows
Never quite believing that their safety's guaranteed
As the river on its journey quietly flows.

Lying in the valley of the West Lyn some 600 feet in altitude and backed by wooded hills, the rebuilt village of Barbrook consists of several stone houses, a red-tiled chapel, a triple-gabled post office and general stores, with the beautiful West Lyn river flowing down the central causeway.

Three main waters go to make up the West Lyn river, an unnamed stream, Thornworthy Water, and the West Lyn itself which has its source above Ruckham Combe 1,500 feet up The Chains and threads its way down through the landscape, meeting up with the Thornworthy Water at Cherrybridge in Barbrook, and then on to the sea at Lynmouth.

Devastation struck Barbrook on the night of the Lynmouth flood disaster on 15 August 1952, when the deep-gorged river rose to a height of 30 feet sweeping away houses and people in its relentless journey of destruction. Individual stories of the tragedy are told in Eric P. Delderfield's book 'The Lynmouth Flood Disaster', one of which was of two young Australian girls on a hiking holiday. Because of the torrential rain they had begged a lift from Blackmoor Gate, and the motorist having dropped them at Barbrook they sought shelter at the nearest house where the lady took them in. It was one of a row of 12 council houses built in 1928, and the time was around 8 o'clock. By 10 the houses had gone, disintegrated into the flood with 12 lives being lost in that row alone. The lady and her grandson disappeared, it is believed, where the road had collapsed into the gorge. The two Australian girls also drowned, their bodies being recovered later.

Beggar's Roost, 1,000 feet high overshadows Barbrook; to the south-east is Stock Castle, an Iron Age earthwork. Another earthwork is Roborough Castle further on, above Hoaroak Water.

The red-tiled chapel

Hillside view of the village ▶

Hillsford Bridge

A bridge that spans the meeting of the waters
Which joyfully resound as they unite,
Rushing over pebbles smoothly weathered,
An everlasting vision of delight.

Enclosed by a grandeur of wooded hillsides and luxuriant scenery, this small hamlet is one of Exmoor's beauty spots where can be seen the confluence of Hoaroak and Farley Waters. The secluded Combe Park Hotel and Hillsford House opposite serve to complete a superb country scene. From its beginning high up on The Chains, a rain-soaked barren plain 1,500 to 1,600 feet above sea-level and the source of many Exmoor streams, Hoaroak Water descends in steep falls eastwards and from the watershed of Exe Plain runs parallel for 5 miles with Farley Water, separated only by Cheriton Ridge, until they meet at Hillsford before joining the East Lyn at Watersmeet. Hoaroak Water was named after the ancient oak tree which marked the boundary of the Royal Forest. The present tree was planted in 1916. The Two Moors Way foot-path on a southwards journey from Lynmouth passes through Hillsford before continuing to Cheriton Ridge.

During the night of the Lynmouth flood disaster in August 1952, a call for help came from Bridgeball, a hamlet ¾ mile from Hillsford Bridge. A fire tender took off from Lynton crossing Barbrook Bridge which was already awash and proceeded to Hillsford Bridge, but when they reached there they could get no further, one bridge was down and the other damaged by the rising waters. Returning to Lynton, the river at Barbrook had overtaken the bridge making it impossible to cross, leaving them stranded between the West and East Lyn rivers.

In 1685, Major Nathaniel Wade, a fugitive rebel from Monmouth's defeated army at the Battle of Sedgemoor, was found by a farmer's wife from Bridgeball, Grace Howe, hiding among the rocks at 'Illford Bridges' downstream from the Howe's farm. She fed and looked after him at her own risk of death.

There is a National Trust car park and walkers can explore the water up to Scoresdown or down to Watersmeet and Lynmouth.

The converging waters at Hillsford ▶

95

Rockford

Steep wooded hillsides rise above
This hamlet's narrow way,
Its river coursing through a glen
That shades the light of day.

Following the road from Brendon on the right bank of the East Lyn, the river widens to about 20 feet across as it tumbles over large boulders towards the rocky gorge of Rockford, a glorious hamlet cleft in its narrow valley of hanging woods and sheer hillsides. A footbridge spans the river to a house almost concealed by foliage, and from which a path leads adventurously along the bank.

Although river paths can be followed all the way to Watersmeet or east to Brendon village, the road after Rockford leads inland and climbs up past Brendon church, leaving the river deepening ever lower in its rocky gorge. Up river leads to Malmsmead bridge straddling Badgworthy Water, the boundary between Devon and Somerset.

At Rockford there is a cluster of pleasant white~washed houses under slate roofs whose inhabit~ ants must be attuned to the lullaby of the Lyn as it journeys its way towards Watersmeet, and seasoned to the shafted and dappled sunlight that pierces and filters through the canopy of branches and leaves.

The 17th-century Rockford Inn sits close to the river and, decked attractively with hanging flower baskets, looks inviting to the thirsty and hungry wayfarer who is looking for a rest and a break as it combines a restaurant and tearooms.

The power for a wheelwright and carpenter's shop built by William Floyd in about 1870 was supplied by a small tributary stream spilling just before Rockford. The rusty remains of the water~wheel and machinery have long been hidden by encroaching undergrowth.

View of Rockford from the footbridge ▶

Brendon

Beneath the rounded contours of the hills,
Through woods of oak, the river flowing by,
The heartbeat of a village never stills
As long as folk their diligence apply.

The historic village of Brendon, meaning 'Bramble Hill', straggles along the valley road between steep rounded moors and the clear waters of the East Lyn before its wild dash to Lynmouth and the sea. The slate-roofed, white-washed cottages of simple design lining the street, together with a sheltered village hall, the Stag-hunter Inn, a hotel, a shop and post office, give it a thriving air, while a triangular village green completes the country scene. It is considered to be an angler's paradise. Often the hunt is seen passing through.

It is a large parish and abounded in Doone legends and the story of Lorna Doone long before R.D. Blackmore wrote his romantic novel based on facts. A path out south over the Tippacott Ridge leads to Hoccombe Combe and the ruins of the medieval settlement of the Brethren of St. John of Jerusalem built in the 12th century, and which, in a confusion of facts, was wrongly attributed to Blackmore's Doone Valley before neigh-bouring Lank Combe was established as such. It was at the old forge in Brendon (now a guest house), close to the packhorse bridge, that Blackmore's John Ridd witnessed the blacksmith stepping outside with the red-hot horseshoes to dip them in the Lyn.

To the south also, through the hanging woods above Badg-worthy Water, the land rises steeply to the carpeted and lonely expanse of Brendon Common where hardy cattle and sheep graze and the wild mealy-mouthed Exmoor ponies wander.

Coming in from the west, on high ground about 700 feet above sea-level, the parish church of St. Brendan (Brendan the Nav-igator and Celtic missionary) stands 1½ miles from the vill-age, having been moved there in 1738 (stone by stone it is said) from Cheriton, a one-time Domesday estate.

Brendon village from the green ▶

98

Malmsmead

A place of tranquil mood, despite the many folk
Who pass through here intent on following the guide,
They dream their dreams awhile, enjoy the old~world charm
Then on, to find Doone Valley and the waterslide.

A mile distant from Oare Church along a narrow winding road, and one comes suddenly upon this lovely hamlet in its idyllic setting, the pulse quickening in anticipation. For it is here that the renowned Lorna Doone Farm can be seen with Badgworthy Water (pronounced Badgery) running under the bridge and is where the luxuriant river walk to the famous Doone Valley profuse with rhododendrons can begin. Once thought to be the Plovers' Barrows Farm where R. D. Blackmore's John Ridd took his bride Lorna, this red~roofed, long white building has since been established by researchers as Farmer Snow's residence in the 'Lorna Doone' story; John's farmhouse proving to be originally on the site of Oare House at Oare.

The Doone Valley itself has been repositioned over the years from Hoccombe Combe, where are the remains of a religious settlement and the probable cause of the confusion, to the nearer Lank Combe valley at the foot of which is the famous waterslide up which torrential slope John struggled when he was a boy, out of curiosity, only to find himself at the entry to the Doones' stronghold. Remains of the 'Doone~gate' can be seen at the far end of Lank Combe. The evidence can be found in Sir Atholl Oakeley's booklet 'The facts on which Blackmore based Lorna Doone', wherein he sets out to put right the wrongful indications of the past. However, the whole area is known as Doone Country.

Surprisingly unspoilt despite the thousands of tourists on the Doone trail, Malmsmead provides a large car park and picnic area. The Lorna Doone Farm itself houses a shop supplying a variety of tasteful gifts and postcards. There are also riding stables in the centre of the hamlet; at Parsonage Farm, where horses can be hired out for trekking; and at Cloud Farm in the heart of the Badgworthy Water scenery and close to the Blackmore mem~orial. At County Gate north~east of Malmsmead on the Devon/Somerset border, there is a tourists' information centre.

The ford and bridge at Malmsmead ▶

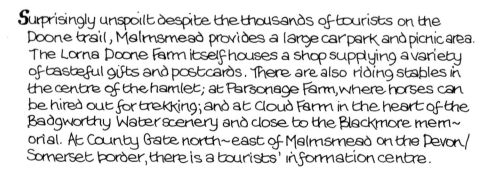

Penny Housden

Oare

Inside Oare Church where Lorna on her wedding day was shot
By Carver Doone, her fortune to him lost,
Imagination re~enacts the outlaw's loathsome plot,
His end in Wizard's Slough was what it cost.

The parish of Oare, on the west Somerset border not far from the sea, is a large moorland settlement of some 4,017 acres, the focal point of which is the church of St. Mary the Virgin, built on rising ground. The original building of the present structure consisting of just the nave and inner chancel dates from the 14th century. The porch was added later, and the tower rebuilt in 1850. On the wall by the door is a memorial tablet to Richard Doddridge Blackmore, creator of 'Lorna Doone', a replica of the one in Exeter Cathedral.

Encompassed by lush green meadows, sparkling streams, and rounded heather~cloaked moorland hills, this delightful little church is of world~wide interest, for it was here that Blackmore's romantic hero, 'girt' John Ridd, wed his lovely Lorna who, seconds later, fell across his knees mortally wounded (or so he thought) ~'the sound of a shot rang through the church and those eyes were dim with death'. And then of his imm~ediate pursuit on horseback after the revengeful Carver Doone, over Black Barrow Down, across the long stretch of moor, and finally a plunge into the black ravine leading to the Wizard's Slough. Here, with both men fighting to exhaustion, Carver stumbled backwards into the sucking black morass and sank from sight. Fortunately, upon John Ridd's return, to his untold joy, he found that Lorna had survived the gunshot wound.

Oare House, across the valley from the church, stands on the site of the original Plovers' Barrows, the Ridd's farmhouse where John took his bride. Oare Manor, which is close by the church, a forbidding grey stone building, has a long and interesting history of heirs who ran the estate over the centuries. To the south~east along the Oare valley past the houses of Oare~ford, where the Lillycombe stream runs into Weir Water is Robber's Bridge, a narrow~structured road bridge 8 feet wide, mistakenly associated with the Lorna Doone story as it was not built until long after the Doone era.

Church of
St. Mary the Virgin

View from the church to Oare House ▶

Stoke Pero

High on a hill, their own creed to follow,
Parishioners live by the land, truly blest,
Their little stone church lying snug in a hollow
Beckons them into its haven of rest.

This tiny hilltop settlement lies remote above a densely~wooded valley and has for 4,000 continuous years been populated by the farming fraternity. Stoke Pero Parish Church is, at 1,013 feet above sea~level, the highest church on Exmoor and the oldest Christian site. It is believed to have had Celtic begin~nings, and the medieval church was probably of 13th century date, of which only the tower and porch remain intact, the latter's doorposts cut from two solid blocks of oak. When it was rebuilt in 1897 a donkey called 'Zulu' earned his place in the annals by plodding twice a day for months between Porlock and Stoke Pero, bearing timber for the new waggon roof. His portrait hangs on the church wall. Of the long list of incumbents who came and went, Rector Robert Thryng, in 1369, fell from grace by kidnapping a woman called Alice from Buckethole, a farm outside the parish border, 'though nothing is known of the outcome. It was not a popular living, giving rise to the couplet: 'Culbone, Oare, and Stoke Pero
Parishes three, no parson'll go.'

In the year of the Domesday census (1086) 76 people were listed in the parish, and by 1881 it was down to 49. Today there are only a few farms and a cottage or two. The public house (now Church Farm) run by the parish clerk, had its licence revoked by the Sir Thomas Acland of the day because the previous landlady had buried two husbands 'near the cellar door'.

Up until the late 1950s the road was still unmade and Stoke people were said to have developed high~pitched voices from shouting to one another across the valleys.

To the west is the Nutscale reservoir into which flows the Chetsford Water that issues out of the high moorlands and runs through a beautiful combe.

The parish church

Church Farm ▶

Penny Housden

West Luccombe

There's something about a country lane
That makes the thoughts come sweeter,
There's something about a village green
That makes the world seem neater.

A lovely tranquil spot within the National Trust's Holnicote Estate (pronounced Hunnicut) with a few old stone cottages, tiled and thatched, one or two colour~washed cream, with names like Rose Tree and Inglenook, a farm, an old~world green redolent of maypole days, and a tiny packhorse bridge straddling the Horner Water which burbles on its way towards Bossington and the sea.

Tucked away behind the trees in an ideal location is a caravan and camping site, and for those who like to ride or trek, a stables hire out horses.

Many enjoyable walks can be taken from the hamlet in a variety of landscape, one in particular being called 'Granny's Path'. It is thought to be named after a member of the Acland family in whose possession the Holnicote Estate resided for 200 years before Sir Richard Acland, the 15th baronet, passed it over to the National Trust in 1944.

Starting from the West Luccombe to Ley Hill road, opposite a house called Luckbarrow, the path leads round the head of Halse Combe, and from there passes below Pentley Seat. Here, a path leads up to the Seat where flagging energies can be renewed and from where splendid views can be obtained.

Carry on until the path meets up with the 'Cat's Scramble'. This is a track believed to be named after a nimble pony called 'The Cat' which belonged to the 12th baronet's wife. When the little packhorse bridge is reached below Horner Green, turn left, whence the path climbs steeply, living up to its name, to join 'Granny's Ride'.

The packhorse bridge

Cottages at West Luccombe ▶

106

Penny Housden

Horner

Oakwoods but a step from the cottage gate
Portraying the beauty of Nature's estate,
Strolling awhile in its leafy domain
Enjoying the freshness of sun after rain.

According to historical findings, the delightful hamlet of Horner lies along the ancient Harepath that runs from the Quantocks to Barnstaple, a route that was used centuries ago by the Anglo~Saxons along which to move men and supplies. It is in fact a Saxon word meaning 'army road'.

This is a lovely part of the Holnicote Estate owned by the National Trust. The cluster of dormer~windowed cottages with flower-filled front gardens enclosed by low stone walls, presents an idyllic picture in summer, with the tiny packhorse bridge leading into the woods. Magnificent woodlands of some 900 acres extend to both sides of the valley, mostly of oak ~ acorns have been renewing the oak-woods of Horner since the Iron Age ~ with a scattering of ash and alder, hazel and holly. Through here flows the Horner Water from which the hamlet takes its name ~derived from the British 'hwrnwr', 'the snorer'. Many walks can be enjoyed from this starting point. Red deer roam the coverts and in October can be heard the belling of the stags. In late summer at Cloutsham Farm~built as a hunting lodge ~ by the great rounded Cloutsham Ball near to Horner, the opening meet of the Devon and Somerset Staghounds takes place.

On the edge of the woods at Horner, in a sheltered spot, is an impressive but disused 3~storeyed water~mill with its 18~foot diameter, 6~foot wide overshot wheel, currently being converted to residential use. It was erected in 1850 by John Clarke, the miller at West Lynch, who was expanding his business. History records the existence of a mill here in the 16th century which prompted a later historian to mention the removal of a fulling mill when 'cloth was tentered on the green at Horner'.

A pleasant car park is set in an old orchard next to a cottage tea~garden. Horses can be hired from the farm.

A Horner lane ▶

The Lower
Tea Garden
& Gift Shop

OPEN

Penny Housden

Luccombe

'The valley shut in by the hills', or 'enclosed valley'. An unspoiled village of infinite appeal nestling at the foot of Dunkery Hill between its sister villages of Horner and Wootton Courtenay. Charming individually-designed cottages of thatch and tile over cream-washed walls face the main lane and continue round the corner into Stoney Street, passing by the little stream that runs at the roadside.

There is a village hall but no school or inn, the only shop is the post office with its thatched beetle-browed roof and stable door. Luccombe's crowning glory is the beautiful medieval church, part 13th century, part 15th, dedicated to St. Mary the Virgin, which has a prominent position above the houses, and whose west tower rises to over 80 feet. The interior is light and airy and has a Jacobean pulpit dating from James I. In the chancel a double piscina (for the priest to wash his hands after the offertory) and a sedilia, or seat, let into the wall for the priest, are two of the oldest features.

Another point of interest is the Byam memorial on the north wall, in Latin, surmounted by the family's armorial bearings. Dr Henry Byam was Vicar of Luccombe and Selworthy. He was also a Royalist supporting King Charles I, and when he was taken prisoner by the Parliamentary forces of Oliver Cromwell's, his wife and daughter attempted to cross the Bristol Channel by boat, but both were drowned. Dr Byam eventually escaped from his captors and rejoined the King at Oxford, but after the King's arrest escaped with the young Prince Charles to the Isles of Scilly, thence via Jersey in the Channel Islands to France. In 1660, after Prince Charles was restored as King Charles II, Dr Byam returned to Luccombe where he died in 1669 at the age of 89.

Approach to this attractive village ▶

111

Tivington

A narrow, rising lane leads to this hamlet
Of farms and barns and views across the vale,
The chapel sits content within its haven
Preserved through centuries of wind and hail.

This is an idyllic hamlet of dispersed farms and cottages tucked into hillsides that face out towards Por~lock Vale to the sea, and across the ploughed fields and pastures to the distant height of Dunkery Beacon. It is a valley of sweeping views and magnificent landscape with a pervading air of country quiet, interrupted by the occasional clip~clop of a passing rider on his horse. For there are enjoyable rides through woodlands and over the open hills.

The focal point of course is the St. Leonard's Chapel-of-~Ease which stands beside the road leading to Wootton Courtenay, a mellowed sandstone building with a thatched roof thought to have been built by Sir Ralph de Middelney (who held the manor of Blackford) in the mid~14th century. It has a large open fireplace. After the Reformation when services ceased to be held it became, in turn, over the next few hundred years, a storehouse, a barn, and later, in the 19th century, a 'dame' school under Mrs Ann Stears, and later, Mrs Jane Kingdom. Behind the altar can be seen the blocked square~headed east window when a cottage was built against it. The vestry is the

St. Leonard's
Chapel~of~Ease

sitting room. However, in 1896 the chapel was restored by the Acland family when services were reinstated, and it was further improved in 1940 by Dr Francis Eeles of Dunster who donated the tryptych over the altar. A discarded box pew from the mother~church at Selworthy was made into a read~ing desk, and the oak pews came from Milverton church. The bell over the door is believed to have come from the Acland yacht, 'Lady of St. Kilda'. St. Leonard's, which is in regular use, is the only church building in the diocese of Bath and Wells to retain the traditional Somerset thatch of wheaten reed.

To the west, at Blackford, there is an ancient stone dove~cote to be seen.

View of Tivington ▶

Penny Housden

Wootton Courtenay

So pleasant wandering down this country lane
With garden flowers sparkling after rain,
An old barn's mellow stone defies its age ~
Another century's tale on history's page.

Known as 'the place in the woods', partly deriving its name from the Courtenays, Earls of Devon, who held the manor in the 12th century, this small village of attractive cottages contains the Old Rectory, an hotel, general stores, post office, garage, and a water~powered mill pottery, turning out fine stoneware, the only one of its kind in Somerset. Wootton Courtenay, on the south~west slope of Wootton Common between Luccombe and Dunster, looks south over field and pasture towards Dunkery Hill, the highest peak on Exmoor, and to the cairn~encrowned hills of Joaney How and Robin How at the base of which, towards Luccombe, is the woodland junction of tracks called Webber's Post, named after Tom Webber of Brompton Regis (1812~1863), a yeoman staghunter.

Set back and rising above the village is the church of All Saints with its great yew tree alleged to date from about 1350. In the porch is a holy water stoup hewn from a single block of stone. There is a fine waggon roof with carvings of the Evangelists, a pelican, St. George and the Dragon, the eagle of St. John. The oldest parts of the church ~ east end of the chancel and lower part of the tower ~ date from 1250, and the rebuilt tower is of saddleback design. Windows and roof-carvings are of the Perpendicular period, the octagonal font is 15th century, the pulpit and pews Victorian. The wooden screens fitted in the chancel and across the tower were carved by local people in 1921 and are of great work~manship. Discovered then was the 'squint' in a blocked re~cess which once enabled those standing in the north aisle to see the altar at the east end of the chancel.

In the old days children picked whortleberries here in summer to supplement the family income, working hardest of all on the last day when they were allowed to keep all the money they earned.

The village street ▶

Penny Housden

SOUTHERN EXMOOR

Southern Exmoor

The Caratacus Stone on Winsford Hill

Wimbleball Lake from Haddon Hill

Dulverton Bridge

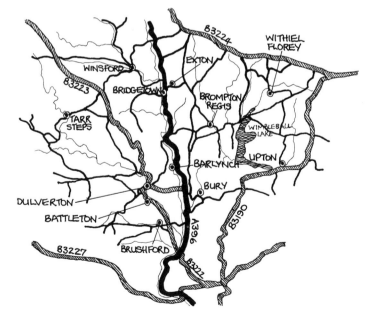

Map for location purposes only

Winsford

*A wide entrancing scene to please the senses,
An ancient green, stone walls, and rustic fences,
Beneath the arcs of quaint historic bridges
Time's waters carve the inevitable ridges.*

This attractive well-set-out village on the River Exe and the Winn Brook, considered to be one of England's prettiest, is notable for its eight bridges over running waters, including a packhorse bridge. Old cottages add their allure. The picturesque thatched and much-photographed Royal Oak Inn facing the green, parts of which originated in the 12th century, has a fine restaurant and 14 bedrooms.

Ernest Bevin, the great trade union leader, wartime Minister of Labour, and later Foreign Secretary, was born in the village on 7 March 1881. His birthplace, bearing a plaque, is across from the post office/stores.

The Old Vicarage, a private house since 1968, is part medieval; the Rectory is of 18th century date; Karslake House, originally a malt house, dates from the mid-15th century; higher up is the entrance to Yellowcombe Lane, an old packhorse track. The old schoolhouse was where Bevin was enrolled at age three.

The parish church of St. Mary Magdalene on The Steep, with its lofty tower and rounded arch stone doorway, has a Norman font, a 13th-century chancel, a large painted panel of the Royal Arms of James I dated 1609, and a peal of six bells.

Ernest Bevin's birthplace

Points of interest in the vicinity are the Caratacus Stone in its shelter at Spire Cross on Winsford Hill, inscribed with the Latin words 'CARAACI NEPUS' believed to be a religious memorial, its first reference documented in 1219; the ageless Tarr Steps in the Barle Valley; and the Wambarrows on Winsford Hill ~ three ancient burial mounds.

The Royal Oak Inn where Tom Faggus the 17th-century highwayman is said to have waylaid travellers ▶

Bridgetown

A passing~through road, a passing~view road,
A short row of dwellings and comfortable quarters,
But step off the high road, into the by~road,
Over the bridge to its tree~shaded waters.

A little hamlet full of rural charm cradled in the valley below Exford going south~east. Here, and running parallel with the road beneath its old hump~backed bridge of a single arch is the fast~ flowing River Exe, 30 feet wide, rippling over pebbles and small rocks and sheltered in a shady, glady nook of bankside willows and alders, sycamore and ash. By the bridge is the disused Methodist Chapel, and there are more cottages along this little backwater.

Between this bridge, which probably gave the hamlet its name, and a second bridge is a large grassed area of a caravan site, facing which is the magnificent Bridgetown Mill, now residential, intact with its water~wheel 14 feet in diameter by 4 feet wide which once powered three pairs of stones. When it was in operation it was one of the largest mills on Exmoor. At this moment in time proposals are in hand to get the wheel working again as a tourist attraction as the whole building and equipment are in good condition, including the leat that branches off to power it. In the 19th century the mill was owned by the Phillips family who also combined the trades of machinist, wheel~ wright, carpenter and smith.

Bridgetown
Mill

The former post office on the highway was once the wheelwright's premises, and the white~walled Badgers Holt Inn, almost opposite, is a welcoming oasis and has its own history of occupation.

The River Exe at Bridgetown winds southwards with the road through luxuriant landscape past the ancient settlements of Miltons and Kents, where there was another mill, under the fine~structured Chilly Bridge and thence on to its con~ fluence with the River Barle at Dulverton.

The old Post Office amid cottages at Bridgetown ▶

Penny Housden

Exton

On the hilly reaches of a valley incline
Householders mark their existence,
Nurtured and thriving like grapes on a vine
Displaying their fruitful persistence.

The hill village of Exton, an old Domesday settlement, was described in the 18th century as 'one of those high parishes that teaches its inhabitants the virtues of industry and frugality from a necessity of nature'. A necessity that has continued for generations.

Houses, hotel, church, and a schoolhouse with a slate-hung wall on its weather side, are built into a steep wooded hillside that overlooks the beautiful Exe valley and the moors beyond, while below can be seen the sleepy hamlet of Bridgetown. And flowing down its valley the majestic River Exe hurries toward its confluence with the Barle. In a bad winter snowdrifts block the narrow village lane.

The ancient stone church of St. Peter's on its lofty mount — whose castellated square tower has been said to be 'the rudest and roughest of its kind in the district' — has Norman traces of origin. The preaching cross in the churchyard was restored in 1875 with Ham Hill stone. Like many others it had been broken at a time of conflict.

The nave, which has a waggon roof, is of 16th century date, as is the north aisle and the windows with their elegant tracery, and the octagonal font is of Perpendicular style. On the north wall photographs of church plate show that the chalice and paten dated 1574 were crafted by the Exeter silversmith Richard Hilliard, father of Nicholas Hilliard miniaturist painter to the court of Elizabeth I.

In the old days at Exton, along with other parishes at the annual 'Revel', 'wrestling of the most brutal order was the game of the feast', and the prize, a beaver-skin top-hat, was placed on the altar during afternoon service to be seen by the congregation.

In a backwater ▶

Brompton Regis

A community raised to the bells of St. Mary's,
Serving, conserving a heritage so fair,
Wherever you wander the scenery varies
Compelling the traveller to 'stand and stare'.

Better known as Brompton Regis this pleasant village is also called Kingsbrompton on account of its early settlement having passed into the ownership of William the Conqueror who seized the 'Manor of Bruntone' after the Battle of Hastings from Ghida, Harold's mother. Later it became part of the manor of William de Saye who founded Barlynch Priory, near Dulverton. 'Brompton' indicates a settlement surrounded by broom, a yellow flowering shrub.

On the extreme southern edge of Exmoor and surrounded by the delightful scenery of Haddon Hill's purple acres, the woodlands of Storridge Hill, and the peaceful Hartford valley, Brompton Regis was at one time the largest parish in square miles in Somerset, with several shops and craftsmen and a sizeable population, even as late as the decade after the Second World War. Today it is a smallish village in a street of terraced cottages and scattered farmsteads, with the ancient church of St. Mary, whose original tower, built 1200, has double lancet bell openings, a Methodist chapel, the white-walled George Inn, and a combined post office and stores, the latter incorporating tea-rooms.

St. Mary's
Church

The River Pulham runs by the eastern end of Brompton village under Rock Bridge, where there is a ford, past Rock Cottages and Pulhams Mill, and joins the Haddeo by the hamlet of Hartford. Pulham Mill once had a water-wheel but was re-built in the early 1980s.

Just above Hartford House and following the Haddeo it leads to Wimbleball reservoir which was designed to fit naturally into the landscape. Completed in 1978 it covers 370 acres and holds 4,500 million gallons of water. Car parks, picnics and play areas are provided, with sailing and fishing amenities.

Cottages and village stores ▶

Withiel Florey

A tree~shaded parish of rustic appeal
  Where solitude beckons and hedges conceal,
Long past are the days when men pitted their skills
To the hack and the hew deep inside yonder hills.

A small parish of a few scattered farmsteads and a church next to Castle Hill Farm, lying a mile or so off the road going west from Ralegh's Cross. The great days of this area were during the last century when the extraction of iron ore from the Brendon Hills was a thriving concern. But prosperity was short~lived when deposits proved limited and too dangerous to tackle and the mining had to cease.

The terminus of the gravity railway which began at Watchet, ended at Gupworthy Junction which lay within the parish at the northern edge where, today, the outlines of the old station house can still be seen, along with the remains of the old track and mine workings.

The little plain church, dedicated to Saint Mary Magdalene, where registers began in 1697, has been altered over the centuries. The tower is partly 13th century and many alterations were undertaken in the 15th. In 1871, on the Feast of the Epiphany, a practically rebuilt church was presented. The chancel and nave had been restored, the pulpit, desk, lectern and vestry, and stained glass windows were all new. The old minstrel gallery at the west end had been removed but the Norman font retained. The tower arch had been elevated.

St. Mary Magdalene
Church

A month after the restoration the whole building might well have been destroyed by fire had not a passing workman noticed smoke belching from the tower and investigated, to find flames coming from a stove that had been left burning to dry out the walls.

By 1958 the church building had become dangerously unsafe and was closed, but parishioners raised enough contributions for its full restoration and it was reopened in November 1961.

Castle Hill Farm ▶

Penny Housden

Upton

Dwellings of Brendon stone and Treborough slate.
Threaded along a high and windy road,
Time was when cattle drovers plied this ridge
And rested up on overnight abode.

With its few houses and farmsteads strung out beneath the windy ridge of Haddon Hill which dominates the skyline, Upton is a small community on the road between Lowtrow Cross with its ancient inn and the expansive waters of Wimbleball reservoir; among the few amenities are a garage, church, chapel, and village hall. The mellowed residence of Bittescombe Manor is north of Lowtrow.

All that remains of the medieval church of St. James's is the tower which, once doomed to demo~lition, has now been cleared from its encasement of ivy and been moved and is preserved in a field beside Upton Farm, a mile to the north-west. The new church that replaced it was built in the late 19th century under the Diocese of Bath and Wells, and has stained glass windows. The little roadside chapel is still in use.

Through the valley meanders the River Haddeo which, issuing from the Brendon Hills, flows through Wimbleball reservoir before it reaches Bridge End at Upton, a rustic stone bridge of a single 3~foot arch which adequately takes the narrowing Haddeo as it flows from its source. The 'eo' of Haddeo and 'don' of Haddon are derived from the Anglo~Saxon for 'running water' and 'mound or hill' respectively.

Beside the bridge in its lovely setting is a cluster of four attractive houses, one called Mill Cottage which presum~ably is on the site of the old village grist mill.

A rumour that went the rounds in the 1930s but was not substantiated, was that a house in the vicinity secreted Charles Lindbergh and his family away from the spotlight after the kidnapping of his baby from his home in the USA.

Cottages at Bridge End ▶

Penny Housden

Bury

A sunset glow, a river's flow,
A cobbled bridge beside a ford,
A quiet place, a breathing space,
To rest awhile in sweet accord.

Two miles east of Dulverton and sheltered in the lower reaches of the Haddeo valley, this picturesque village of old cottages and converted dwellings has the lovely River Haddeo flowing through its centre. Down by the ford it runs 30 feet wide on a shallow bed, though it can get deep, where traffic can cross 'downstream, not straight'. The long narrow packhorse bridge spanning the river beside it is four-arched and leads to the other half of the village.

Turning into Bury village the buildings to the left were once a row of shops, including a butcher's, and what was once the Methodist church, built in 1889, is now a house. An inscription on it reads 'Preach the Gospel to every Creature'. Opposite, the house with the steps was once the village hall.

Back to the ford and across the packhorse bridge, the first house called 'Cowlings' has a Victorian postbox set into the wall, and to the left is the old schoolhouse/Anglican chapel-of-ease, built in 1890 and now residential. The road to the right follows Lady Harriet's Carriage Drive, constructed at the end of the 18th century and named after Lady Harriet Acland, wife of Col. John Dyke Acland. This was in acknowledgement, so the story goes, of her brave action in going up the Hudson river in an open boat and rescuing her wounded husband who was held prisoner by the French in the American war. Towards the beginning of this bridlepath, near Pixton Park, can be seen the motte and bailey of Bury Castle, a medieval fort which guarded the entrance to the Carnarvon Estates.

A footpath in the village leads to Haddon Hill from where there are grand views to Wimbleball lake and beyond.

Bury ford by the four-arched packhorse bridge ▶

Brushford

A quiet retreat far from the multitude,
 The river winding by,
The old church stands in noble solitude
 As timeless as the sky.

The lovely countryside in which Brushford is set gives it a quiet air and a peaceful one, enhanced by the silver Barle running close by. In this sheltered valley old stone cottages dream in the sunlight and the fine medieval church of St. Nicholas lies wrapped in past ages on its grassy knoll, in its church~ yard an ancient oak that has seen some 800 summers.

The church has a few treasures. A 12th-century Purbeck marble font bowl, an early 16th-century alms box still serving its original purpose, a beautiful rood screen, circa 1460, unusually~designed silver candlesticks on the altar, an old oak chest that was hollowed from the trunk of a tree. The porch was rebuilt in 1725 with its old ironwork retained.

The Chapel of St. Mary the Virgin, dedicated in 1926, and built in memory of Col. The Hon. Aubrey Herbert, soldier and scholar, was designed by the renowned Sir Edwin Lutyens. It is reputed that John Buchan based his character Sandy Arbuthnott in his novel 'Green Mantle' on Aubrey Herbert.

St. Nicholas
Church

The disused Dulverton railway station is in the parish, now converted, once on the Taunton to Barnstaple line, as is the Carnarvon Arms Hotel which is still thriving. This was built in 1873 as a railway inn but was always popular with the fishing fraternity. Opposite the hotel, a few fields apart, the rivers Barle and Exe hurry to meet each other at Blackpool, a quiet junction.

Lying north-west of Brushford is Combe House, a Tudor mansion, the seat of the Sydenham family from 1540 to 1874. A cousin of the family, Elizabeth Sydenham from Monksilver, was the second wife of Francis Drake.

Looking out on a quiet lane ▶

Battleton

Passing through the gateway to the age-old moor
  This long meandering road is but a glimpse before,
The varied scene, regardless of opinion,
  Enfolds a world of multifarious dominion.

Following the route from Brushford, Battleton lies along the approach road into Dulverton, a long string of houses on either side, some of them quite old. Further along on the left, where Andrew's Hill slopes down to the junction and sheltering beneath the backdrop of tree~clad hills, is Battleton House. This is a white 18th-century building that was the home of Dr G.F. Sydenham from 1861 to 1924, a medical man, and a member of the notable and respected Sydenham family.

A little beyond Battleton House, on the right, is the recreation ground with its shelter, formerly a cattle pound for stray animals. This was presented to the village in 1920 by Charles Hardcastle Abbot as a memorial to those who perished in the Great War 1914~1918. A path alongside the River Barle called Pound Walk leads up to the five~arched Barle Bridge at Dulverton which is believed to be more than 200 years old.

Pixton Park in the vicinity, a large 18th-century building with Victorian alterations, was the West Country seat of the Herberts (Earls of Carnarvon) which came into their possession by marriage in 1796, and which Aubrey Herbert and his wife Mary, after their marriage in 1910, made their permanent home. Because of his love for Pixton the house had been presented to him in 1901 when he became 21.

During the 18th century Pixton House in its deer park was the ancestral home of the Aclands. This is where the bridle path starts that is called Lady Harriet's Drive and which runs parallel with the River Haddeo all the way to Wimbleball Dam.

Battleton House ▶

Dulverton

The river runs a moat around the hills,
A magnitude of trees on castled heights,
No drawbridge this that leads into a town
Of pleasant scope, steeped in ancestral rights.

Lying just inside the southern boundary of the Exmoor National Park, crossing the five-arched stone bridge over the River Barle, this small town is known as the 'Gateway to Exmoor', and at one time was a popular meeting place in the staghunting season when the town would spill over with huntsmen and their followers. It was also a centre for fishermen with the Barle uniting as it does with the River Exe further south.

Old inns like the Lion, which hostelry is still in existence, had their animal emblems depicted on their portals, and the prestigious Town Hall is an important feature. At the lower end of the town is Exmoor House, once the workhouse but now the headquarters of the Exmoor National Park; the visitors' centre and Heritage and Arts, is higher up. To the forefront is an engaging bronze statue of the young Lorna Doone in 17th-century dress, sculpted by George Stephenson of Exeter, commissioned by the late Dr Whitman Pearson of New Hampshire, USA, who was President of the Anglo-American Lorna Doone Society.

Town Mills

It was in Dulverton that R.D. Blackmore's John Fry took John Ridd, the boy, into an unnamed hostel 'with the air and grace of a short-legged man and shouted "Hot mootton pasty for twoo trav'lers, at number vaive, in vaive minnits! Dish un up in the tin with the grahvy, zame as I hardered last Tuesday".'

At the church of All Saints one of the eight bells is purported to have come from Barlynch Priory, and some of the stained glass was presented by Sir George Williams who founded the YMCA, a man of whom the town is rightly proud.

Dulverton's Fore Street ▶

Barlynch

On sacred ground between the river and the road,
 A farmhouse stands where once religious brethren prayed,
Its borrowed stones remain a testament to faith,
 Transcending quietude itself, all fears allayed.

Some two miles north~east of Dulverton, in the wooded valley of the River Exe, a farmhouse, barn and cottage now stand where once Barlynch Priory housed its community of Augustinian canons. This small religious order, founded in the 12th century by William de Saye, Lord of the Manor of Brompton Regis, numbered only six canons and their prior and possessed few assets.

A letter written by the King's Commissioner, Dr Tregonwell, to Thomas Cromwell, Henry VIII's minister, after his visit to 'ye religious house at Barlyche in Somerset' reported 'A house of Chanons of thordre of Seynt Augustyne ... I perceive that the Prior of that howse will be and is content to resyne his rome and office of priorschipe ... The howse is in dette £40 and yn some rewen and dekey.'

Before the Reformation the Priory ran a little school for novices, taking in one or two outsiders, and recently there has been found part of a Latin notebook used by a pupil who attended there.

When Barlynch Priory was closed and destroyed in 1537, during the dissolution of the monasteries, 13 tons of lead were stripped from the roofs and sent to the Mayor of Bristol for the King's pleasure. Many of the Priory's relics ended up in parish churches in the area.

Today's farmhouse and buildings, occupying the same site as the old Priory, have incorporated in them its re~ maining stones. With the river running serenely alongside, and the deer sanctuary in Barlynch Woods, the setting remains as tranquil as it ever was in the days of the brethren.

St. Nicholas Priory state ▶

Tarr Steps

Tread reverently across the wide expanse of timeless waters,
A legacy of permanence to all our sons and daughters,
Echoes from an ancient past lie hollowed in the wind,
Stepping stones of antiquity link futures unimagined.

The age of this unhewn stone clapper bridge, or causeway, spanning the River Barle on the road from Hawkridge to the ridgeway over Winsford Hill, has never been established, but it is scheduled as an ancient monument under the Office of Works. Some archaeologists believe it was constructed during the Bronze Age on account of the round barrows discovered along trackways, others that it is medieval and built at about the same time as the clapper bridges on Dartmoor. Local legends ascribe it to the work of the devil. What is indisputable is that the bridge was a great engineering feat in a machine-less era that has endured and will continue to endure over countless centuries.

Consisting of 17 spans without a fixture of any kind, supported by piers 4~6 feet apart, 3~4 feet high, and about 3 feet in breadth, and with raking stones piled either side sloped to break the force of water, the length of the bridge from bank to bank is 135 feet, extending to 180 feet over the Hawkridge road.

The bridge has sustained damage from time to time. Once in the flood of 1939, and again in the iced~up winter of 1940/41; when the thaw set in, accompanied by heavy rain, the whole of the middle section was destroyed. Temporarily repaired it was not until 1949 that it was properly reconstructed. Then in 1952, at the time of the calamitous Lynmouth flood, all but one of the clapper stones and its piers were swept away. It was not until June 1953, under the aegis of the Somerset County Council, that the stones, which had been widely dispersed, were gathered, and the bridge rebuilt.

Tarr Farm

At Tarr Farm, on the east side, there is a restaurant and tea~rooms for visitors. Thought to be 16th century, the farm has a stone~built circular staircase rising from the kitchen.

The ancient stone clapper bridge ▶

Penny Housden

WESTERN EXMOOR

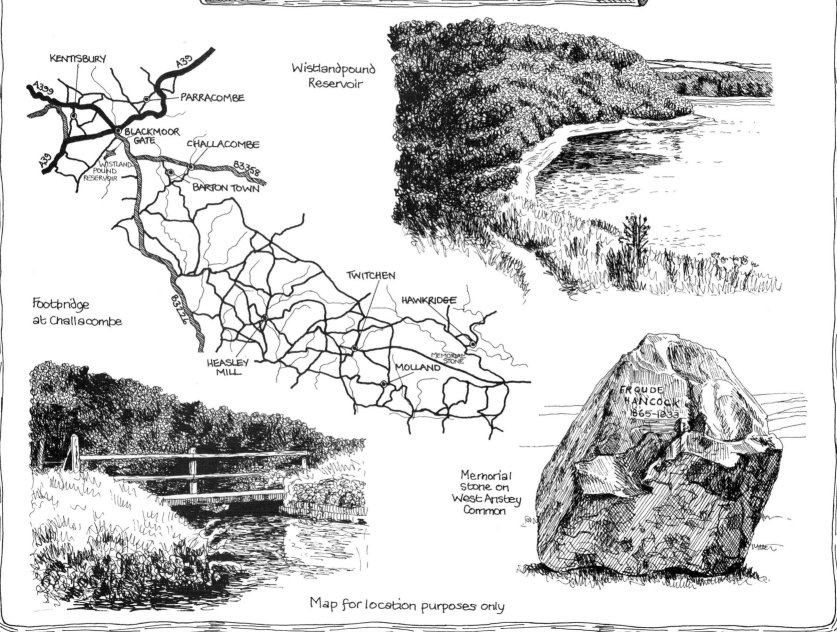

Western Exmoor

KENTISBURY

A39

A399

PARRACOMBE

BLACKMOOR GATE

CHALLACOMBE

A39

WISTLAND POUND RESERVOIR

B3358

BARTON TOWN

B3226

TWITCHEN

HAWKRIDGE

HEASLEY MILL

MOLLAND

MEMORIAL STONE

Wistlandpound Reservoir

Footbridge at Challacombe

Memorial Stone on West Anstey Common

FROUDE HANCOCK 1865-1933

Map for location purposes only

Hawkridge

High~ridged, this is a cold spot on the moor
  Where wild winds bluster round the cottage door,
The old old church which silently endures
  Stands testimony to their overtures.

One of the oldest settlements on Exmoor built 900 feet high on a wild and windy ridge, Hawkridge is blessed with few houses and the ancient parish church of Saint Giles which stands in lonely vigil with lovely views from the churchyard across to Anstey Common. Thought to date from Saxon times because of its nearness to the ancient roadway across Tarr Steps, the church has a Perpendicular tower rising to a height of 1,000 feet above sea-level. The Royal Arms of Queen Victoria appear over the entrance to the chancel, dated 1877, the font and south doorway being of the late Norman period.

At the foot of the ridge, below Tarr Steps, there are rich woodlands where the River Barle and the Danes Brook converge, while in the Barle Valley but now overgrown are the Iron Age forts of Brewer's Castle and Mounsey Castle. The Two Moors Way, a long~distance footpath between Dartmoor and Exmoor, passes through Hawridge and follows the Barle Valley on its route north to Lynmouth.

On West Anstey Common there is a memorial stone to P. Froude Hancock Esq. (1865~1933) subscribed to by 500 of his friends which marks the moorland boundary.

Saint Giles church

Hawkridge, and Withypool, another ancient settlement in the heart of the moor, have always been closely associated because of their joint relationship with the Royal Forest since the days of the Saxons, having 52 Free Suitors between them. These were small farmers permitted to keep their holdings inside the Forest to whom certain rights were acc~ orded. In return they had to provide services as required by Forest laws such as rounding up sheep, cattle and horses 9 times a year, and attending the two Swainmote Courts.

Village houses ▶

144

Penny Housden

145

Molland

So restful just to wander through the lanes
And feel the heartbeat slow to nature's pace,
To breathe a sigh for all things manifest
And let antiquities reveal their trace.

Molland ~ its Celtic name 'bare, round-topped hill' indicating its remote past ~ clings to the southern slopes of Exmoor albeit a little outside the National Park confines, and basks in an air of peace and tranquility. One of the quiet country lanes leads to West Molland Barton, home of the Courtenay family. In the mid ~18th century this manor house had been leased to the Quartly family who became known for their Red Devon cattle.

In the centre of the village amenities include a post office and bakery and the oak~beamed London Inn, reputed to be 700 years old and a favourite haunt of summer visitors.

On a grassy knoll overlooking cottages is the unspoilt church of St. Mary's of mostly 15th century date, its tower base and font dating back to Norman times. Features of interest include the 18th century 3~decker pulpit and canopy, the horse~box pews, and a striking Georgian screen. A plaque in the wall gives an instruction, in the event of Napoleon invading in 1804, 'The "conductors" of local wagons are charged with taking the "Sick and Infirm" to safety while keeping off the King's Highway and breaching if necessary any hedges with "proper Tools".'

It is said that R.D Blackmore (of Lorna Doone fame) based Parson Chowne in his novel 'Maid of Sker' on a former in~cumbent of St. Mary's, the infamous Parson Froude who had a tyrannical reputation.

In 'Lorna Doone' Tom Faggus the highwayman brought his bride Annie (John Ridd's sister) to live in Molland where he had purchased 'a nice bit of land'.

The London Inn

The cottage lane to St. Mary's ▶

146

Twitchen

A farmstead cluster in a moorland setting,
A weathered church nestling in between,
High~banked lanes to combat the elements,
Shelt'ring its brood from the outward scene.

Enfolded in the contours of the moor, and from the higher Cussacombe Common appearing isolated but independent, Twitchen is an old farming community passing down through generations. The name means 'the meeting of the two ways' and was, in the old days, at the junction of two pannier pony and pack~men trackways and therefore a welcome resting place. The cluster of mellowed stone farm buildings on the hilly lanes seem to close in on themselves.

Because a settlement grew up here a place of worship was a natural progression, and a church was built dedicated to St. Peter. It still retains the original Norman font, and all but the tower was rebuilt in 1844. Several generations of families are buried in the churchyard including the Lyddons who owned Twitchen mill which is no longer operating, having been converted into a private dwelling. Many Lyddons were prominently active, one William drove the first stage wagon from Minehead to Bristol, and later espoused the Methodist cause along the southern edge of Exmoor; another William, an expert craftsman, operated his many skills around the various farms in the district and left a diary of his activities to his descendants.

St. Peter's Church

The school house, once the centre for children from outlying farms, no longer functions, having also reverted to private use.

For the visitor there are now Twitchen Wagon Tours arranged in the summer season, one starting at Cussacombe Post with a pair of shire horses on a round trip of eight miles taking about 3 hours including a picnic stop, and one starting at the Sportsman's Inn, Sandyway, with a team of four horses, visiting an historic public house, the Royal Oak, at Withypool.

View from Cussacombe Common ▶

Penny Housden

Heasley Mill

Grey slate roofs on colourwashed homesteads,
A worn iron plough on a patch of green,
The old mill~stream on its endless journey
Ripples its way through the changing scene.

The sleepy air encompassing this quiet, attractive hamlet on the River Mole, belies a once bustling community which in its heyday was surrounded by working mines. Bampfylde mine alone, just north of the village, the largest of them all, employed some 200 men, and records show that from 1860 to 1881 almost 5,000 tons of copper ore were extracted, valued at over £48,000, and £4,000 of iron ore. A tramway was built at Brinsworthy Bridge, a mile to the south~east of Heasley, to carry the ore down to the railway at South Molton, the remains of which can still be seen. For recreation the miners would hie to North Molton 3½ miles distant to spend their hard~earned pennies at the Miners Arms, an inn which still exists. Their noisy but easy camaraderie can be imagined as they strode along dusty lanes.

As the output fell and the mines became uneconomical they gradually closed, and by 1900 mining had ceased. An attempt in 1939 by a detail of Canadian Royal Engineers to re~open the mine at Florence, a mile eastwards, proved unsuccessful.

For centuries before the mining era Heasley had a thriving woollen trade, and tannery, one of the mills alongside the river being four storeys high, but by the middle of the 19th century the industry had foundered.

Today, the old mine shafts lie concealed in the undergrowth. The few cottages that are left make a pretty picture, the old Methodist chapel still opens its doors, the little school serves as the village hall, and the whitewashed hotel beckons to the stranger. An old iron plough on the village green is a reminder that agriculture also played its part in the scheme of things.

The turning into Heasley village ►

150

Penny Housden

Challacombe

High in a combe where the winds blow cold
Round many a fire old tales are told,
Though times hold up in a changing world
The village bides in a past unfurled.

The old English name of this moorland village means 'cold valley' situated as it is 1,000 feet up and open to the prevailing winds. A mile-and-a-half to the east is the Edgerley Stone which marks the Devon/Somerset boundary. This roadside community of cottage homes includes the attractive 'Black Venus' inn. This was previously called the 'Ring of Bells' but was known as the Black Venus once before in 1812. The name reverted back in 1845 when the bells were rehung in the village church of Holy Trinity high up at Barton Town a mile distant.

The River Bray flows under the road west of the inn where there is a ford by a house and an old wooden footbridge. Alongside the stream is the Methodist chapel built in 1868, a packhorse bridge that was erected in 1843 to replace a wooden one, and the disused schoolhouse. The former rectory is near Rooksfoot Bridge. The flooding of the Bray during the storms of 1952 caused much damage to the road.

Positioned a mile above the village is Challacombe Reservoir, the smallest of Exmoor's 3 reservoirs (the others being Nutscale and Wimbleball), covering just under 4 acres with a capacity of 11½ million gallons, built mainly to supply Ilfracombe.

The Black Venus Inn

Reminders of ancient man abound on the surrounding hills. To the south-east the ramparted earthwork of Shoulsbury Castle; to the north-east the burial mounds of Chapman Barrows, Longstone Barrows and Wood Barrow, and the impressive 9½-foot high slate menhir of the Challacombe Long Stone. Not far from the boggy depression of Mole's Chamber is the Sloley Stone, erected in 1742 to mark the boundary between High Bray Common and Gratton Manor Common. The stone once stood at the head of Lew Combe further to the north.

Challacombe ford ▶

152

Penny Housden

Barton Town

It's strange to think that there are always others gone before
  Who lived their lives, and dreamed their dreams, and asked for little more,
Ancestral voices may be stilled, yet make themselves be heard
  In every whisper of the wind, in each recorded word.

In splendid isolation atop a windswept hill, and approached by a long, beech-hedged lane rising to a height of 900 feet, Barton Town with its small but sturdy group of farm buildings and parish church seems to have grown out of the very soil beneath. Seen from across the valley it has been likened to 'an embroidered motif stitched into the velvet of the hills'.

Holy Trinity church with its square castellated tower, and affording entry through a slate-roofed lych gate, has a plain interior with a 14th-century font and serves its home village of Challacombe about a mile away. One can only wonder at the fortitude of past congregations in getting there in good weather, never mind inclement. In dense moorland mists visiting curates on horseback would find the church difficult to locate and were often late, straining the patience of the waiting parishioners who were eager to return home to see to their Sunday dinners. The churchyard is filled with the graves of the hamlet's forefathers, one bearing the name of Edward Webber, a famous local wrestler, buried in 1847 at the age of 102.

Further down the slope where Challacombe Mill House now stands is where the original corn mill once ground its meal but a little nearer the lively River Bray by which it was fed. The last miller here was a Mr Huxtable who was born in 1881. The leat still trickles past a short row of old cottages before rejoining the Bray. The bridge just below is of course known as Mill Bridge.

The area abounds in wild life, and there is much evidence of early man on the surrounding hills in the form of tumuli and burial mounds.

Barton Town in its setting ▶

Parracombe

Of narrow streets and valley steeps
Embraced by moorland, combe, and stream,
High on its hill in ancient splendour
The little church transcends the dream.

Built on the steep sides of the valley the village rises to a height of 1,575 feet at the south-east end where, at Churchtown, the treasured church of St. Petrock lies in peaceful seclusion. It is of ancient foundation with an unspoilt Georgian interior of high box-pews, a three-decker pulpit and a musicians' gallery. The walls of the square tower are 8 feet thick.

By the 1870s it was considered unsafe and in 1877 a new church was built nearer the village centre. Despite talks of demolition for the little church it was eventually considered to be of historic interest. The restoration was celebrated with a packed congregation on Trinity Sunday 1972 with music from a string quartet taking their places in the musicians' gallery. The two old cottages beside the churchyard used to be the ale house serving beer to the worshippers. Church and alehouse were linked as meeting places.

Christ Church is in the early decorated style and is built from stone quarried locally. Seen from the church porch across the valley is the motte and bailey of Holwell Castle which was built in Norman times. Another feature of interest is the henge (a sacred site) on Parracombe Common, near Woolhanger, dating from 2,000 B.C.

The River Heddon runs under the stone bridge at the bottom of the village where are a number of cottages and the Fox and Goose Inn that was once roofed with thatch. Until recent times there was a corn mill, a brewery, bakery and shoemaker.

Parracombe used to be served by the Lynton to Barnstaple narrow-gauge railway which operated from 1898 to 1935.

The ancient tower of St. Petrock

A wintry scene on Parracombe Hill ▶

Blackmoor Gate

A welcome moorland wayside inn
  Where tourists flock to wine and dine,
But once a thriving railway station
  On the Lynton~Barnstaple line.

An oasis in the moorland landscape open to the winds and weather. A few scattered houses and The Old Station House Inn on the site of the old railway station; southwards lies Wistlandpound reservoir.

At one time moor gates were in existence wherever a borderer used his right of common, and the gate at Blackmoor was a little to the south of today's crossroads. Their purpose can be recognised by a distinct change from farmland to heath.

When the Lynton to Barnstaple railway line was constructed, between 1895 and 1898, the station at Blackmoor Gate was a stop for excursionists exploring the western moor. The narrow-gauge (slightly under 2 feet wide) single track line ~19 miles long ~ was considered more suited to the hilly terrain than standard-gauge, and on 11 May 1898 the first train ran the course at a statutory 15 miles an hour passing through some beautiful scenery and following the contours of the hills. There were 4 engines: Lyn, Taw, Exe and Yeo, and 16 coaches. The fare was 3s. 3d third class, later reduced to 2s. 3d; Lynton to Blackmoor Gate cost one shilling. In 1899 stables for 20 horses were built at Blackmoor station, and during the summer season a four~horse coach service was run to Ilfracombe. Sadly, the line proved unviable, and the last train carrying 300 'mourners' ran on Sunday 29 September 1935. Blackmoor Gate station was bought for £700 by a Mr T Brown who built a hotel nearby but which was destroyed by fire in the 1970s.

Today's inn with its colourful sign and its welcome façade, with the original signal on the green in the forefront, is a bright, inviting place to halt for a meal.

The Old Station House Inn with original signal in foreground ▶

Kentisbury

No village wares or general store
  To bind the folk to country lore,
Yet still tis bound in history
  With stories wrapped in mystery.

Lying about two miles north-west of the modern crossroads of Blackmoor Gate, Kentisbury is a small parish 600 feet up on the edge of the National Park. Like most of the upland churches St. Thomas is built of a dark, slatey stone, the battlemented tower a fine example of late 15th-century construct~ion. The church was restored and enlarged in 1874~5, and regarded by some as a spoilation. On the wall is a long list of rectors who had served the parish during different reigns, and the length of their incum~bencies, some of them for a considerable number of years ~ from a William Ballomy who first built the parsonage house and died in 1566 in the 8th year of Queen Elizabeth's reign, to John Richards the 3rd who succeeded his father and rebuilt the parsonage house in 1720 in the 6th year of King George the 1st's reign. Printed below is the following :

  'These men have been the Rectors of this Place
  Who Preach'd the Word of God and taught his Grace
  Happy had been their hearers to attend
  To their instructions and their Lives to mend.'

Church of
St. Thomas

A later rector, the Rev. Thomas Openshaw built a school in 1877 to accommodate a hundred children.

The Barton, close to the church, is of stone build with a slate roof and a tall fronting chimney, and has a date stone of 1685. Patchole and Bridwick in the vicinity were Domesday estates, and on Kentisbury Down at 1,105 feet there are a number of barrows and prehistoric remains.

By a patch of green stands the War Memorial to the soldiers who died in the Great War.

The Barton ▶

Exmoor ponies near
Malmsmead Hill

Index (page numbers in *italics* refer to illustrations)